# Mosaic

# Mosaic

✦

## A Child's Recollections
## Of the Russian Revolution

*Valentina Antonievna Seletzky*

iUniverse, Inc.
New York  Lincoln  Shanghai

# Mosaic
## A Child's Recollections Of the Russian Revolution

iUniverse, Inc.

For information address:
iUniverse, Inc.
2021 Pine Lake Road, Suite 100
Lincoln, NE 68512
www.iuniverse.com

ISBN: 0-595-30408-7

Printed in the United States of America

# Contents

# REQUIEM FOR THINGS REMEMBERED

There was—there was—and there was not—a land of snows and white birches—of golden wheatfields and soaring skylarks—of jeweled church domes and old dwellings called "terems"—of primeval forests and sleepy hamlets—of flower-studded meadows and vast endless steppes—of fabled rivers like the Volga and the Dnieper—and God was over all!

There were—there—and there were not—windows of old estates flung open to seas of lilacs and "cheremukha"—the poignant moonlit concerts of the nightingales—the wail of the village accordion at twilight—the lonely bells of the troikas braving the silence of frozen lakes—and God was over all!

There are—there are—and maybe there are not—ghostly young voices rustling in the aspens and the willows—shades trailing wisps of shrouds over the marshes—abandoned hollow-eyed izbas with cold empty hearths—and snowflakes, pristine and pure, drifting endlessly over the crumbling old crosses of a forsaken graveyard—and God is still over all.

# REVOLUTION

My first realization that something unusual and very terrible had happened in Russia occurred one day while I was sitting on the floor of our salon and drawing a picture of an imaginary "firebird." I had heard the word Bolsheviks many times, but it had no meaning for me. Suddenly my father rushed in and took my mother into his arms. He whispered something in her ear and she broke into tears. Immediately I was gathered into his arms and our small family went to our Russian church.

As we approached I noticed that the courtyard was filled with people, mostly on their knees and crossing themselves frequently. When we entered the church everyone was either crying or praying. One large man near us in the blouse of a peasant was on his knees bowing his forehead to the ground again and again. One heard sobs and the frequent "Bozhe moi" (My God!) again and again. When I looked at my mother's pale face she whispered, "The Bolsheviks killed our Tsar!"

The slight white-haired priest of the church held up his hand, and clasping his cross to his heart, began to speak in the silence that followed. Some of his phrases must have entered my heart to stay there forever.

"Imagine," he said in his mild voice while tears filled his eyes, "imagine our Tsar—our Gosoudar—standing holding his ailing son in his arms."

The Tsar, or Gosoudar, as we called him, was our link to God. I had been taught to pray for our ruler ever since I had been taught my first prayers. I, too, began to sob, perhaps not fully realizing what had really occurred. I remember our family kneeling and that I had a premonition that it was a horrible occasion. The nightmare that we would endure seemed to hover over us.

The priest's voice ceased—he could no longer speak. The congregation to a man remained on their knees while the icons of the saints looked down on the stricken crowd with a steady gaze of compassion, sadness and some severity.

My memory takes me back to those times in sort of a mosaic of adventures and events.

# SNOWS OF RUSSIA

No deep snows that I have ever seen in all my years in America have ever brought back the memories of snows in Russia. The remembrance of Russian snows is never evoked by snowfalls experienced here. Sometimes after a winter storm someone would ask me, gazing outside, "Doesn't this remind you of Russia?" It never did, and I don't think it can. Even when I had waded here knee-deep in snow-drifts and listened to the muffled sounds of the city, even when I had driven through the snow-covered country-side of Midwestern plains, it was all different, and far-removed from the winters of Russia.

The snows of Russia were different. Under Russian skies they created a unique world, blotting out the realities of everyday life, changing completely not only the surroundings but also a way of life for weeks and months. It was a descent of a mighty and mysterious monarchy to subjugate, to impress with a magnificent grandeur, to impose an imperial kind of majesty.

There was a smell to the snow—and indescribable cold fragrance of which one was conscious. It tickled the nostrils, grazed the cheek, and glued eyelashes together momentarily.

As a small child, let out into the courtyard for a daily "constitutional," I remember these snows Small I must have been but yet the walls of snow cleared on either side of a pathway, rose like mountains above me. And wandering between them I felt the isolation of being in another world. These walls of snow, towering above, did not intimidate me. I felt alone, but I was not afraid. As I recall, a large kitchen spoon was always in my mittened hand, and with it I would scrape at the frozen walls, dig into white mounds, attempting to do something, to build something. Why the spoon? I do not know, except that I always wanted it when I went out. I was conscious of the blue and purple shadows crated by the mounds, and of the silence, which hung over everything.

I remember falling snow—of seeing snowflakes float down on the dark material of my coat. They were large and patterned, of exquisite, unbelievable designs—no two alike. And they did not melt all at once. They lingered to be observed and examined. I have not seen snowflakes like that in my years here.

I played in the snow. I don't recall whether it was "dry" or "wet."—It was always the kind one could do something with. If one made a small ball of it and then began rolling it, it became bigger and bigger until one did not have the strength to roll it any more. Here they build snowmen, all to the pattern—over there they built "snegurochkas"—legendary snow maidens, and castles and snow-dragons.

One unforgettable sensation is that of the blue-purple shadows cast by snowy drifts, another is of snow in the sunlight.—The brilliance, the rainbow pinpoints on the tree branches, on the fence-posts and everywhere.

Then there is also a sound unlike any other, of someone walking through snow—the crunching shuffle, like biting on a bit of rock-sugar candy. And speaking of candy, there is the unforgettable cold taste of the forbidden icicle plucked from some nearby protrusion, and the fragile musical tinkle as it shattered. Silence—the beautiful mysterious blue-purple silence of the snowy world around me. Sometimes peering into the frozen barrel of water I would see imprisoned lacy designs and would wish to preserve them forever. I don't recall of anyone being with me at those outings. Surely my time outside was supervised, but all I remember was being alone. The walk between the snow walls was unforgettable.

I remember, too, a ride in a sleigh across a frozen river. It must have been in Omsk. Yet what I recall most vividly were the times when I was alone wandering about with my kitchen spoon in hand. Somewhere, too, there is a dim memory of being taken to a frozen pond where there was public skating. There were chairs on runners, and music, and a house called "grelka" where people retired to warm themselves. I remember holding on to a chair and pushing it around. I was too small to skate.

It was in the month of November, after being away for a half-century, that I returned to Russia and encountered snow again. The old town of Tver, halfway between Moscow and St. Petersburg, was deep in snowdrifts, and great flakes floated down from the grey skies. I studied their miraculous designs on the sleeves of my coat, allowed them to pile on my lashes, breathed them in and tasted them for a few enchanting moments I became again the child of those long-ago Russian winters.

# OF CHRISTMAS

When did the magic disappear and the tinsel become tarnished? When did the Great Star fade from the heavens and the untrained young voices of village carolers trail away into silence? I have come to dread the Christmas Season that is thrust upon us earlier and earlier each year so that the stores may have their orgy of sales, the television its orgy of music and shows, and the youngsters their orgy of greed.

It was not always like that for me—some of the best and most meaningful Christmases were under adverse conditions. One of them was in the Cattle-car of our eschalon as we fled from the Bolsheviks. The adults celebrated Christmas by putting up a very small tree and trimming it with chains from old newspapers and cutouts of snowflakes and stars. It had no glitter, but it blazed with a special glory for the children.

Another memorable Christmas was in our early years in America—the little tree in Mrs. Collins' rooming house where we occupied a single room. That tree was brave with tinsel and decorations from the five-and ten.

I was too young to understand the significance of the festivities at holiday time in Russia, but my parents spoke of the Christmas Eve supper consisting of twelve traditional dishes served on a straw-covered table, of the carolers making rounds with a star-topped wand, balls given by my father's regiment, sleigh rides on frozen rivers and the rounds of parties and visits that went on for days. Among the young girls it was popular to revive the traditions and superstitions of fortune telling—"a wonderfully frightening experience," Mama recalled. Some procedures involved peering into candle-lit mirrors set up at angles, or melting wax to see what shapes would form to reveal one's fate, or tossing a slipper out of doors to determine the direction from which one's "intended" would come, and many other similar amusements, some of which are mentioned in Russian literature. I understand that my Grandmother could tell fortunes with cards, but was always reluctant to do so, claiming that "what will be—will be."

The equivalent of Santa Claus in Russia was "Dedushka Moroz"—Father Frost—who owned no reindeer or assisting elves, climbed down no chimneys, but merely walked around with a huge sack on his back delivering goodies and toys to deserving children.

A custom that prevailed widely throughout most of Russia was the gilding of walnuts and using them as ornaments on the Christmas tree. Special little books of gold and silver tissue were obtainable for that purpose in stories. The walnut was prepared by sticking a bent toothpick or wire loop into its head, tying on a bit of colored yarn by which to hand it, dipping it into a cup of milk, and then wrapping it into a tissue leaf of gold or silver. Petted and left to dry, it became a traditional ornament. As quilting "bees: were held in Early American homes, so were gatherings "to gild the nuts" in Russian homes before the advent of Christmas.

The tree itself, of course, was the main decoration and center of attention. It was ornamented with glittering baubles, gold and silver paper-maché toys—the likes of which I have never seen since—with elaborate Victorian bonbonniers holding candy, marzipan fruits and flowers, gilded walnuts, chains of beads and colored candles clamped in small holders to its branches. The lighted candles turned the tree into a magnificent symbol of what Christmas should and could be. They were about five inches high, and the effect of their living flames against he dark green foliage is hard to describe, except to say that those who have seen it are ever grateful for the memory.

As a young child I was taken to some children's parties where the children, led by an adult, danced in a ring around the tree, and where presents were later distributed. I suppose I had a large share of the presents, but I don't recall them except for one. It was an exquisite doll's tea set, carved of wood and painted with crimson mushrooms. Years later, abroad, I saw a replica of that lovely tea-set, and it was almost a traumatic experience to something out of my childhood and to realize that the same pattern of toy was still being made.

Very early I yearned to imitate my mother's embroidery skills, and one Christmas in Omsk I was gifted with an apron to be embroidered in simple outline stitches, skeins of floss and needle being provided. I must state that whenever I expressed a desire to sew or embroider, a needle had to be first "prepared" before I was to have it. Its point had to be blunted with a hammer, and then it was considered "safe" for me to use. The design on the apron that I was given depicted a fox striding along, bearing on a should-stick a knotted kerchief from which protruded a pair of chicken-legs!

In Omsk, on our street, there was a neighboring family with four girls. The youngest, Olia, was about my age. The others already attended the gymnasium and were most sophisticated and condescending. Their last name was Kounnos and the father had some high post in the civil service. "Our papa is a Minister," they loftily informed people. Olia and I played together and I envied her a houseful of sisters and a good-natured mother who seemed happy to Cater to them all. I was invited to their house for Christmas and given an elaborate candy-filled bonbonniere. Olia was in turn invited to my home and given something my mother made. I think it was a lace pinafore.

From my Grandmother in central Russia now came to Omsk her "posilki'—parcels sewn in canvas cloth containing lengths of fine linen, laces, and other items for sewing and handwork, which could not be obtained in Omsk. The "posilki" were certainly different from our present-day brown-paper parcels. They were encased in sturdy cloth, sewn with strong thread, and addressed in purple indelible ink. Some particular materials wee directed by Grandmother to be made up for me into towels and pillowcases. I suppose she was thinking of my future "dowry." To this day there remains a length of hand-woven linen with my name pencilled faintly on one end.

While actual images of the Russian Christmases are very faint, there remains a feeling of a most distinct and special atmosphere—a magical kind of an aura, which descended and permeated the season for a brief while. As I said before—when did the enchantment fade and the tinsel tarnish?

# DOLLS, TOYS AND MISHKA

Since I was the only child, the only grandchild, and the only niece—the relatives were generous and I had many toys and dolls. The best of dolls at that time came from Germany and France. Many other toys were also imports.

I am told I had a doll I called "Mimishka"—after Mimi, I presume. It was a French import with a body made of soft kidskin. I can't remember her at all, only that the kidskin body captured my imagination and I repeated frequently that I, too, had a kidskin body.

There are toys and dolls I do remember—

A kind of plaster medieval tower. All white, with battlements, about a yard high, with colored stained glass windows. A condole place within lighted it up magically. Since this could only be done by grownups, it was not much of a plaything. An uncle gave it to me, and it was much admired by the family.

Another useless plaything was the "Easter Table." This was a foot-and-a-half replica of a dining table set with traditional Russian Easter foods in miniature. The dishes holding various Easter goodies were firmly molded to the table and the platters held Easter hams, poultry, tall Ester breads, cheese paskhas, and miniature bottles of wine and champagne. Everything was reproduced in true colors, the miniature feast looked most appetizing—what it was made of I do not know. It was a display to be looked at, not played with, since nothing could be removed. The grownups admired it also—to me it was nothing.

There was a large toy goat coated with real fur, mounted on wheels. When its head was pushed down it bleated. It was nearly life-size. There was also a cow on wheels, covered by real cowhide, smaller than the goat. It had a little tape near the udders, and when that was pulled the cow could "Moo-moo." I don't know if I was enchanted with these animals. They were expensive and admired, but how could one play with them? They were good props for the playroom.

Unfortunately most of my dolls were named by the grownups that gave them to me. My indifference to dolls I think stems from the fact that I had little to say about them.

My aunt Mura, Mama's sister, who was a bit overbearing, gave me a beautiful blonde doll dressed in red. Already the doll was called "Katia." I had her for a long time, but was never particularly fond of her. She was a large doll about a yard high, face made not of porcelain, but a celluloid-like substance. Not particularly pretty. Two small red bows were fastened in her hair—she wore a fine wool dress, pleats in the skirt, girded by a satin bow.

There was also a large boy doll called by the grownups "Volodya." He was dressed in a green velvet Lord Fauntleroy-kind of suit with a straw hat on his head. An Edwardian kind of a doll. I never played with him much, as I never played much with other dolls. I recall that he was in our baggage as far as Chita, Siberia, and my father sold him to some toyshop there. I never missed him.

There was a porcelain baby doll whose German-made head I still possess. The very short hair was made of plush, very life-like. I liked him best, but the grownups had a name for him, "Baylis"—and it could not be changed. For some reason he afforded much amusement to the family and I felt that I had no claim on him. This take-over by the grownups had much to do with turning me off where dolls were concerned.

Now so with Mishka! That one belonged to me wholly. No one came between us. My father bought him to me after World War I, and I opened my arms and my heart to him as to no other doll or toy. While he was a stuffed bear, he was my constant companion, my confidant. Somehow we were left to our own devices, and it was recognized that Mishka was my very own special possession. The undisputed stamp of ownership was marked early, and no grownup played with him or even handled him. No one joked about him, and it was generally agreed that he had the most "intelligent" expression. He was entirely MINE! My careful handling of him despite inseparable companionship must have been unique for so young a child. I was never destructive—all my toys testified to that.

Mishka went with me everywhere and wore some of my clothes. In those early days he was golden-colored and my hair matched his. I resented any rough handling of him by others, and I don't recall that any other child was allowed to play with him.

When we were escaping from the Bolsheviks during the Revolution, he was packed with some family belongings into a trunk. When that trunk was lost—stolen, really—my grief knew no bounds. The recovery of that trunk later brought great joy. In those turbulent times when people fled for their lives, when all possessions were left behind, or scattered in flight, the recovery of that one trunk was a miracle indeed. I contained the cherished five piece silver sterling coffee-set, my father's precious cigarette case, some needlework of my mother's, family photos, and, of course, my Mishka. All these things were the treasures of our home in America.

It is my belief that Mishka was the guardian of that "treasure chest" just as he has always been guardian of my welfare, past and present. I find comfort in his black-button eyes in my dark moments. He guards my home, and when the time comes he will be laid to rest at my feet, so that I need never be alone.

# PASTRIES AND SWEETS

Paper-thin wafers embossed with Austrian Imperial seals came stacked in large round tins. I am told they found great favor with me. I called them "Albertiki," and was never denied one. They were the size of a tea-saucer, and must have been very bland and perfectly harmless. Perhaps an "Albertik" appealed to me because of its size and shape, rather than its taste.

Of the rich and fanciful pastries procured from the top "conditorie," I have a dim recollection of "French horns"—a delectable pastry filled with fresh sweetened whipped cream. I think I enjoyed blowing into one end to see the cream come oozing out, although I imagine the practice was discouraged. (In later years I was delighted to find the "horns" in Denmark, and could not resist blowing out the rich cream, although my antics scandalized my dinner companions."

With the advent of spring it was the custom to bake "javorniki"—skylarks. These were of sweet dough, shaped in birdlike forms with raisins for eyes. Grandmother always baked them and ceremoniously presented me with the rosy fragrant image of a bird, which I abstained, from eating for a long period of time, not wanting to destroy it.

The parents often spoke of wonderful pastries sold in some first-class confectionery shops and bakeries in Zhitomir, and how it was customary to order special "tortes" for different occasions. Tortes were not only for birthdays and name-days, but were sent to friends to celebrate just about anything—advancement in one's position, a move into a new house, and anniversary, an engagement. Any theme was catered to. When my aunt completed some advanced university courses giving her a certificate to teach in higher schools, her friends sent her a torte on top of which rested an open book with an inkwell and a plumed pen, all made of marzipan, chocolate and sugar.

There was a torte called "Mikado" popular with the family. It had layers of crispy sweet wafers between an almond filling. When cut, it looked "frosty," according to my father who loved it.

It was in Omsk that I knew; my mother to have an interest in baking, since grand mother was always in charge of the household in Zhitomir. But grandmother was now long miles away, and although there was a cook in our kitchen,

Mama tried her hand at culinary arts. The absence of those famous pastry shops in Omsk prompted the wives of the regiment to develop their own skills. One of Mama's accomplishments was "honey cake," which for some reason I disliked, but she also made "sand-cookies" and meringues, which I adored.

In Omsk, living in an entirely separate wing of our large house, was an elderly couple. The woman, wife of the overseer, very motherly, extremely kind, sometimes baby-sat with me when Mama had to be away. Her own children were grown and she welcomed the opportunity to be with a young child. I do not recall her name, but I remember her affection. She used to make me "booblichki"—hard, like pretzels, which I loved. I watched her roll out the dough, shape it into rings, throw them into boiling water and then spread them on a sheet for a few moments of oven baking. When they were dry and rosy enough she strung them on twine and hung them around my neck.

"Booblichki," "boobliki," or "soushki," as they were known in Siberia, were common throughout Russia. Sold at bazaar stands and always strung on lengths of hemp twine. Every Russian province had a specialty. Vlasemsk, for instance, was fabled for generations for its "prianiki"—cakes. I just heard of them, never had any.

The berry-pies—gooseberry, currant, blackberry, etc.—had a storybook look about them. I saw their counterparts later in Scandinavia. The difference in the flour made for a most subtle and distinct taste. Something in their appearance plunged me deep into childhood memories. I had seen them sometimes in old still-life paintings, and in later years I tried to emulate their appearance in my kitchen. They always elicited much admiration, but I think they fell short of the real thing.

I don't recall much about candy. As a child I liked sweets moderately, but was never greedy. There was a barley-sugar of many flavors, very popular, called by the Russians "mompassie." Later I learned that they were derived from French candies of the 18th century, which were all the European rage, and which, in French, were called "mon passion."

European marzipan was somewhat different in Russia, not as sickly-sweet as I found it later and its almond flavor was not overwhelming. Shaped into fruits, flowers and vegetables, it adorned Christmas trees, candy-boxes and subtly flavored some pastries. Its use was special and restrained, which made it a real delicacy.

Then there were sugared nuts and large glazed balls of nuts. I don't recall having those. They were probably doled out sparingly, considered "harmful" to children's teeth.

Mama tells of spending the night at the home of some classmate. She must have been nine or ten at the time. As a special treat after supper, she and the family" children were given each a ball of glazed nuts with admonitions not to "crack them with their teeth." After a few minutes during a spirited romp, Mama's "ball" slipped out of her mouth and was lost. She was much put out, but being a very polite little girl and mindful of her manners as a guest, she did not say anything about it. A couple of hours later, while undressing for bed, she found that it had slipped under the apron of her school uniform and was stuck in its folds. She said that she "sucked on it quietly half the night in bed," enjoying it to the utmost.

European candy-boxes were lavish and over-decorated affairs, with interior flaps of paper lace and small gilded tongs. They still exist everywhere in Europe and may be found here in more exclusive stores.

# WEDDINGS

When my Uncle Vanya, Papa's younger brother, married a sixteen-year-old girl called Dina, I attended the wedding somewhere in some church. Of the bride and groom and the ceremony, I remember nothing. But in the church, on the back pews, there were florists' boxes full of roses. My grandmother lifted me over the box of the pink ones, and over the box of white ones so that I could smell them. I had never smelled roses before.

Later on, there was a party at the house. Someone played the piano and sang and my mother tucked me in bed while my Uncle Vanya and his new wife came to say goodnight.

Aunt Dina was young and pretty and very loving to me. She called me "malish"—little one—and petted me and gave me an 18th-century fan, which I have to this day. It has ivory sticks and a silken tassel, which, she told me, was the hair of Chinese mandarins. Uncle Vanya is a memory of someone jolly and young. I hardly remember him at all.

When we were in Harbin, Manchuria, on our way to America, many wartime weddings were performed in the church. Whenever possible I was present. Many of the brides were Red Cross nurses, marrying Russian officers. They usually wore their uniforms, and their Head Nurse—a dignified elderly woman—was usually the guest of honor. Sometimes, however, the bride wore a traditional gown and veil caught up with orange-blossoms of wax, and then the wedding was a real treat. I was an avid and earnest observer, noticing every detail, enchanted by the beauty of the filmy veil, the gleam of a satiny gown, the stray curl escaping the piled coiffure. The brides always seemed very lovely to me, and in the surrounding attendants I would sometimes recognize former brides. They always seemed to be from the Red Cross contingent.

I knew the wedding service by heart. In those day I learned to read the Slavic script, and could quote verbatim the Biblical passage on the wedding at Canaan:

Go back, go back my memory. Listen to the child mouthing the words after the minister.

"Vo vremy ono—bil brak v Kanye Galileyskoy—"

Why do I want to weep about it all now?

# THEATRE AND MOVIES

My first theatrical experience was in Omsk. "Puss in Boots" was being staged one glorious long-awaited afternoon, and having been on my best behavior ever since I learned that I was to attend that performance, all my thoughts were on that special event. Of the city theatre itself I remember very little, save that it was a vast expanse of rows upon rows of people with children, and that there were gilded box-like structures along the walls, within which more people sat. Everyone seemed to be looking at a gigantic red velvet curtain at one end of the great hall, a curtain that had ropes and tassels of gold looped over it in a fanciful design there were several crystal chandeliers overhead, and when they dimmed, the enchantment began.

The red velvet curtain rose upon a scene of castles, such as were seen in fairytale books but there were no actors on the stage. They came through the audience up the center aisle, marching up the steps to the stage. There was the old kind in ermine robes and crown, with a lighted stub of a candle planted on his bald spot—there was the fabulous white Cat, booted and spurred—there were courtiers, and beautiful ladies in sweeping, glittering gowns. It must have been well staged and lavishly detailed for theatres in those days took their profession seriously, and catered to selective audiences, no matter if the performance was for children or for an adult group. There were many delights and audience participation for the children. In the middle of the performance, for instance, when the CAt is escaping from his enemies, he leaps into the audience with a cry "Children, save me!" and runs up and down the aisles, disappearing magically, then popping up in a gallery above. Actually there must have been half-dozen white cats let loose in the theatre among delighted, screaming children who reached out to touch the furry shapes and they sped by. The happy pandemonium reigned for a few minutes, then everything settled down to more fairytale enchantment.

The performance of "Cinderella," my second theatrical experience, is remembered for moments of visual beauty. There are things about this particular fairytale performance which have remained with me throughout the years.—When Cinderella goes to the ball, for instance, she wears an airy gown of blue-green sequins and clouds of tulle. As I have always had a strong response to blue-green, I wonder if the first sight of that marvelous shimmer imprinted its beauty on my mind for all time?

There is also a memory of an intermission during which I was taken to the promenade in the foyer of the theatre. I was fascinated by the sight of so many children walking around with their elders. They were beautifully and elaborately dressed—frilly lacy dresses, small heads of curls, bows and silken sashes—their costumes amazed me. I do not think that I was as dressed up, although I am sure I was wearing my best outfit.

At home I dreamed over the performance, acted it out in my solitude, and always the beauty of the blue-green sequined ballgown haunted my imagination. Blues and greens were always the colors toward which I veered, the colors with which I lived later on, and which dominated my palette.

In Semipalatinsk, later on, there was a public garden with an outdoor theatre. Performances there were; mostly vaudeville type, and I saw a few. I remember a huge man dressed as a woman who sang a song about cornflowers in a high falsetto—at the end he would give out with a deep bass laugh, and display a booted leg from the folds of his satin gown. He was a great favorite, and the audience cheered his antics. Also, there was a very lovely gypsy ballet with gypsies singing around their campfire, while a slim dancer whirled around with her tambourine. It was danced to the popular song of the time "My Campfire," which I now attempt to translate:

> Through the mist my campfire glimmers,
> Sparkling embers upward fly—
> We will steal away together
> To the bridge to say goodbye.
>
> Throw my shawl across my bosom,
> Let its fringes intertwine
> Like the love that was between us
> In another world and time.

I think my love and fascination for the theatre was born in those early days. In later life I put my heart and soul into amateur theatricals, studied the history of the theatre, and designed stage sets and costumes. And always, always I loved that special moment when the house lights dimmed and the great curtain gave its first quiver before rising.

It was also in Omsk that I heard the words "moving pictures" and saw for the first time people moving upon a huge screen.—A memory of black and white shadows, making gestures, moving their lips without sound.

In Semipalatinsk I saw the first movie that I can recall in some detail.—A young girl of an aristocratic family was abducted by an oriental potentate. In the beginning she was courted by him and he lavished gifts and attention upon her, which flattered her. On one occasion he sent slaves to steal into the bedroom of her lodging and decorate it with garlands and sheaves of flowers while she slept. As she awoke and saw her transformed room, I remembmer the words on the screen, presumably spoken by her—

"Ah! This surely must be from him."

Later, as the epitome of innocent young maidenhood, complete with a white dress, white hair bow and white slippers, she was abducted (not unwillingly) and brought to the potentate's court. The command was then given—

"Take her to the harem!"

What followed I don't remember, except that the Oriental splendor faded and real homesickness took over, and finally she was returned (a virgin still) to the bosom of her family. A most touching scene showed the return of her own garments to replace the oriental robes, and as she beholds and recognizes her former dress, she picks up and ecstatically kisses her small white slippers. That maudlin, wonderful, drippy act delighted me.

Another out-and-out melodrama was seen in Harbin with my father. It was about a man involved with another woman, the painful break with his family, his inevitable remorse and the suffering that followed. Driven by guilt and misery, he flees into the country where he meets up with a gypsy who insists on telling his fortune—

"Ah, Baron, Baron! You were born under a fearful star!"

Nothing to do but commit suicide, which he does upon a picturesque bridge. Meanwhile, back home, the abandoned wife is consoled by a wealthy family friend.

Curious, how those first impressions cling to one's memory throughout the years!

# GRANDMOTHER

Her name ws Maria Fedodorovna Kappel and she was Mama's mother. The Dowager Empress, mother of the last tsar, was also a Maria Feodorovna, and that pleased me very much since I loved them both.

I have a last picture taken of grandmother in Russia before all our correspondence came to an end. I am said to resemble her—same bone structure, same eyes and short nose. In the photo she sits wrapped in a lacy shawl, some lace on her hair, and she looks observant and serene. I don't possess the serenity, but it has been said that I, too, am very observant.

This was a very great lady without arrogance or hauteur, elegant and confident in an unobtrusive manner. The kind of person who could roll up her sleeves and knead dough alongside of her cook in the kitchen, and later graciously welcome a high-ranking official in her drawing room. Babushka!—the saintly-to-me woman who later wrote beautiful letters from the Soviet Union, never admonishing, always assuring me that her prayers to the "Queen of Heaven" were on my behalf. I was her only grandchild, and she loved me dearly, that love crossing continents and oceans remained with me throughout the years.

She ws of my build—small. Also a very creative person. Whenever some craft came to town she joined the group to learn. She made fanciful hats when there were; millinery lessons, and paste-colored slippers when a shoemaker came to teach his craft. She sewed, embroidered, knitted, and managed a household of young people who adored her and brought her their problems. In her youth she was said to be lovely, in her old age she was beautiful. Her life's sorrows intensified her beauty.

I was completely in her care during my very early years. There was a nurse, but Grandmother was in charge with constant attendance. Mama was young, and the regiment life with my father made many demands on her time. Grandmother encouraged my parents to fulfill their social obligations. Her own husband—my grandfather—had a government post which often sent him travelling, and so Grandmother became the heart of our family, and the bond between us was strong indeed. Without ever raising her voice or indulging in any dramatics she was the strongest member of the household. I recall that my father said that he was warned by his comrades about mothers-in-law before he married.

"Mothers-in-law indeed," he comments—"There was never anything except warm affection and understanding between us." He goes on to tell of some regiment banquet honoring high-ranking officials, where a toast after toast had to be proposed and downed to the last drop.

"Impossible to abstain, you understand—so glass after glass, as toasts were proposed—starting with the tsar, and going down the line. I came home at dawn in a terrible state, reeling, but aware of my condition. I could not possibly enter the house or the bedroom. So, I went behind the barn where I was copiously and humiliatingly sick. As I was retching, you grandmother came out the back way, without saying a word and held my head, put cool damp towels over it, and presently helped me to a spare room to sleep it off. Not a word was said afterwards, the incident was never mentioned. When I went to kiss her hands, she just smiled and waved me away."

I remember many things about Grandmother. Once she brought back from a farmer's market a pair of guinea pigs for my amusement. "Sea Pigs" they were called in Russia. They were kept in a little pen by the kitchen hall and played with under supervision.

I am told that I had a velvet bonnet with clumps of cherries on one side. The cherries were glazed with lacquer and stuffed with cotton. When I tried to eat them the glaze cracked and the cotton swelled in size. As I was choking and literally turning blue, Grandmother walked in, calmly reached down my throat and removed the cherries. She really saved my life on that occasion. It is reported that she met every domestic (and sometimes foreign) emergency with great calm and presence of mind, but like the true blue-blooded lady that she was, she did faint away once when a mouse ran out of a frilled lace bodice of a gown that had been stored in an armoire.

We were all together as one family until my father was appointed head of the Military School in Omsk. When we left for Siberia, Grandmother remained with my Aunt Nura, Mama's older sister. I think the separation was very painful for all family members. With growing unrest and changes brought about by the Revolution, it was uncertain whether or not we would ever sbe reunited. It had been such a happy, close-knit family, thoroughly enjoying each other's company, sharing each other's interests. There was; my father's young brother, Uncle Vanya (Ivan) with his young and delightful wife Dina, there was my mother's older sister Nura with her doting officer husband, and there was also Mama's younger brothers, an officer—Uncle Kolia (Nicholas) who was as yet unmarried. Over this youthful crowd Grandmother presided like a queen. She arranged their festivities, advised them when necessary, loaned them "family jewels" (there were not many) for special occasions, and was never happier than when the entire house seemed full of young people as they gathered together for various holidays.

"In every room somebody is kissing somebody," Mama once overheard her say. And in my later years, in my own solitude, I pictured the household of young married couples, teasing each other, snatching kisses, rushing at Grandmother to include her in their happy abandon.

As we made our departure to Siberia and Omsk, I have a dim, dim memory of a slight figure standing on the steps of the house, bidding us farewell. In the age-old gesture of despair, she threw a handkerchief over her face, and that is my last memory of her.

In Omsk we corresponded frequently, also in Semipalatinsk. When the Revolution made it impossible to have contact and we found ourselves eventually in Harbin, then Japan, and finally in America, we tried to establish contact through the Red Cross, and eventually were able to receive and send letters.

During our years in America our correspondence was not very frequent, but steady. I wrote frequently, giving the news of the family, our life here, abut my school, and about my own doings. In the early days Mama corrected my letters, then later I wrote on my own, more freely. My Aunt Nura always replied, writing of their life in the Soviet Union where she had the post of a teacher in a Soviet school. Letters were somewhat guarded—one had to read between the lines. However, through the years of early schooling, into high school and beyond that into art school, my letters described our life and my endeavors. At intervals Grandmother would include a beautifully written letter.—Never did she admonish me, always there were prayers that I would succeed, would gain my goals, would find a happy life. My aunt was more pedantic, grown bitter under the Soviet regime, but Grandmother continued to send on her blessings, her prayers, and her hope that all would "turn out well." I felt that a strong bond existed between us. I longed to pour out my heart to her, to tell her of my problems, my frustrations, my early first love, much as her children had done in the old days.

I grew up. I went away to work in New York. One day I returned home to find a black-bordered envelop standing against a fruit-bowl.

Letter from my aunt—long, detailed, bitter. Grandmother had died with the latest picture of me in her hands. Dried flowers from her casket were included in the letter. I have put them in the frame with her photo.

Maria Feodorovna Kappel—a very great lady.

# PAPA

There were three brothers, sons of Maria and Vassily Seletzky. Constantine, the eldest, eventually became the Russian Embassy priest in Washington, DC. The middle one, Anthony, my father, chose a military career, as did the youngest son, Ivan. All three brothers graduated first from the clerical seminary in Volynsk, as it was the whim of their parents to have them become priests. The seminary gave them a rich classical education, but Constantine, always serious and dignified beyond his years, was the only one who became a priest. Graduating with high honors, he was ordained, married a young ward of a distant relative, and wass ent to America where he did well up to the Revolutionary period. Papa and brother Ivan pursued army careers, Papa doing exceptionally well, and both became officers. Papa distinguished himself in World War I, was decorated for bravery, and his star in the military rose from time on.

Papa spoke of his parents as landowners, not too affluent, but comfortabley well off. There was their village of Kolodno, for which he had great love and which featured in many of his reminiscences. He spoke of the Kolodno home as being "a typical country house," because a very large old lilac bush near one wing was the domicile of a nightingale who had built his nest there and returned to it season after season. "Unusual to nest so close to a house," Papa always commented. "And what concerts! What concerts we were priviledged to hear night after summer night."

He seemed to have been closer to his mother, and described her as an exceptionally wise and lovely woman whom he revered. Once, when I had drawn a picture of the Annunciation, taking pains to make the Blessed Virgin very young and comely, he praised my drawing and said thoughtfully, "My mother was like that—as I remember her."

She died before they were grown to full manhood, but he recalled many things about her from his boyhood. He was the inventive one, the one who read voraciously, loving historical romances, folklore and legends. He entertained her, acting out various tales. He made dragons and monsters of straw and twigs, and ensconcing his mother in a chair by the entrance, fought them valiantly for her.

21

She was his Dulcinea, his Queen of Love and Beauty, and she went along with his fancies, laughing a little, but always tolerant and loving.

Not a photograph of her remains—perhaps there was never one taken, but I visualize her—a slender lovely woman looking tolerantly at her young son slaying his straw dragons.

"She was wise, so wise," Papa would tell me. "The village women would come to her for counsel. You know what I heard her tell them several times? 'Guard your modesty, be prudent—never reveal the naked knee!'" That phrase—"never reveal the naked knee"—for not losing one's head in wanton actions. That quaint, old-world expression remained with me, made me pause and think sometimes—words from a grandmother I had never known passed on to me. I wish I could pass them on to someone—but who in this knee-bared sex-crazed world of today would ever heed them?

Papa frequently spoke of her, how competently she conducted the household, greeting the arriving sons from the seminary on holidays, packing them off again with loads of parcels and holiday treats that lasted them for weeks at their seminary.

Her name, like my other grandmother's, was also Maria, and I wish I knew more bout her. Anyway, I had the heritage of two beautiful grandmothers. Of Papa's father, Vassily Vassilitch, I knew very little—he remains a remote figure. There is a little photo of him sent to my father in American by someone, with the notation "Died 23 of July, 1925." On the back there is a scribbled inscription in his hand, "To Anthony Seletzky."

There was also another distant relative, a Natalia Mihailovna, who had a large estate not far from Kolodno. She came from an old noble family, was the widow of the general-governor of the province, and in her youth had traveled widely through Europe. She lived in semi-retirement on her vast estates, engaged in much charity, and kept her eye on the three young men in Kolodno. Her ward, Antonina, a young and pretty girl was married off to the elder brother, Constantine, and went to America with him to establish a family there. Natalia Mihailovna extended her affection all three brothers, but it was Papa who visited her most frequently and spent many of the holidays with her, bringing his youthful exuberance into her solitary domain. Her estates were legendary and her residence luxuriant. Papa spoke of a park laid out in the classical English manner, of the mansion more like a castle, of Natalia Mihailovna herself—a slim, elegant Edwardian figure. She lived in splendid solitude and arranged rabbit hunts and fox hunts for his holidays and gave him splendid horses to ride. He repaid her hospitality by affection and deep respect. He amused her, teased her, spent hours listening to her reminiscences, and became very dear to her.

After his mother's death many of the holidays were spent with Natalia Mihailovna, and he tells so many stories about his visits there. Not having any children of her own Natalia Mihailovna adopted a distant orphaned relative and brought her up as a daughter, educating her in the best European finishing schools, marrying her off to a wealthy personage later, and lavishing affection and attention upon her. The young girl, however, did not fulfill the expectations of her benefactress. Shallow and self-centered, vain and grasping in character, she evidenced little appreciation or gratitude. From time to time, restless and bored, she would quarrel with her husband and descend upon Natalia Mihailovna for a brief visit. Papa remembered one of those descents, which coincided with one of his visits.

"No, she was not attractive—petulant, with a sneering expression, snobbish, unpleasant to the servants and not even very respectful to Natalia Mihailovna herself. She had a passion for taking baths and would sometimes come to the formal dinner table in one of her Parisian negligees."

"For your benefit, naturally?"

"Naturally—and I think it afforded some amusement to dear Natalia Mihailovna. I had never seen before such rich and provocative gowns, but the total effect was like having a potato wrapped in priceless lace!"

Since the lady found no response to her obvious overture she cut her visit short, and Papa was requested to escort her to the train, which would take her back to Paris.

"It was zero weather, the carriage was cold and I was shivering in my overcoat—but she—she lolled back in a long jacket of goose-down, laughing at my discomfort; there is nothing warmer than goose-down, so you will please remember that."

After she was gone Natalia Mihailovna organized a fox hunt for Papa. It is not known if any foxes were run to earth, but there was an elaborate supper afterwards with all participants of the hunt present, and a sixteen-year old daughter of a near neighbor—"an enchanting minx with blackberry eyes"—entertained Papa with her antics all evening—while Natalia Mihailovna looked suitably smug.

Natialia Mihailovna must have been in her late sixties at the time, but she had a much older sister living with her in one wing of the mansion. This lady appeared only occasionally at dinner, preferring to have it in her own apartments, and she was also almost totally blind. However, she knew her way around, and when she did dine in the formal dining room with the rest, she required no special help. Papa remembers how, when fish was served, she carefully delegated the bones to one side of the plate and ate so "daintily and delicately," that it was a pleasure to see.

One memorable visit of Papa's was on New Year's Eve, when he arrived in a sudden snowstorm. Some festivities were cancelled, and they all retired early, feeling a little melancholy. Around midnight Papa was awakened by a knock on his guestroom door. Hastily throwing on his overcoat he opened the door to reveal the night-clad figure of Natalia Mihailovna bearing a large silver tray with a bottle and glasses. Behind her, in similar voluminous night-attire loomed her ancient sister. The two ladies made their way into the room lighting it with the candelabra, which the sister carried. The tray was rested on a bedside table and Natalia Mihailovna poured sparkling champagne into crystal glasses just as all the mansion clocks began striking midnight. Papa said it was an unforgettable sight—the two elderly ladies, night-capped and shrouded in white, toasting with him the New Year, while their grotesque shadows danced on the paneled walls.

On another occasion, spring vacation this time, he was in the flower conservatory with Natalia Mihailovna. Some teasing arose, he dropped on his knees before her—"I will not get up, Natalia Mihailovna, unless you retract your words!" She laughed, and like a young girl went down on her own knees.—"Neither will I get up unless you retract yours!" And so they knelt in front of each other laughing heartily, and it was thus that the horrified elder brother Constantine found them, having just arrived to pay his respects. He thought they both had lost their minds, and later chastised Papa for "unbecoming behavior." He was also a protégé of Natalia Mihailovna, but his dignified mien was something of a barrier, and she much preferred Papa's boyish informal ways.

"Entertain the old ladies, do!" she would appeal to Papa, as she sat with her sister in her sumptuous drawing room after dinner. It was aroom to romance in, Papa recalled: Venetian mirrors reflecting the candle lit sconces, beautiful eighteenth-century French furniture gracefully grouped, curios and precious bibelots garnered from all over the world in cabinets and on small marquetry tables, delicate tapestries and paintings in gilded frames. Fans—and more fans everywhere.

"Oh, what a collection she had of those! Exquisite museum pieces they were, painted and spangled, as delicate as cobwebs!"

Warmed by a glass of excellent after dinner liqueur, Papa would launch into tales and pranks of his seminary school or his military school, sending the two ladies into gales of laughter until they clutched their corsets and begged for mercy.

They also enjoyed the story of how Papa ended his art career.

"I was not the worst in the drawing classes, but my desire was to paint in oils. Oil painting, however, was taught in the upper classes, and only the advanced students were privileged to handle the media. I watched them with great envy, thinking of what I could do with a palette of glowing colors. In the seminary art classes the oils were used for the painting of icons, and some very talented students worked on images of various saints. I particularly admired the almost completed large icon of St. Nicholas—the penetrating eyes fascinated me. One day I found myself in the studio alone and examined the icon minutely. At closer range it seemed to me that the left eye of the saint lacked some luster, and as the paints and brushes were nearly, I unhesitatingly dipped a small brush into a glob of white paint and touched up the area. I set out to correct things, but the harder I tried the more grotesque were the results. The once penetrating eyes were obliterated, the work of the artist ruined by my clumsy attempts. Of course, I was literally booted out of the studio, placed on bread and water fare, et cetera, et cetera. So ended my venture into the world of art."

I must say here that even if he never again touched paints, he had a most astute understanding and keen appreciation of the arts. His encouragement and interest in my creativity, the sacrifices made to promote my own art training and his pride in my accomplishments, spoke for the extraordinary character of the man that was. I owe much to his discerning taste, his drive, his unfailing optimism and enthusiasm.

And so he entertained the picturesque old ladies and chose to be in their company, and, I think, learned much from their old-world graciousness and culture. Later, as a young officer, revealing the name of his fiancee to Natalia Mihailovna, he accepted from her a charming little old watch to present to his Alexandra, and still later a fabulous old necklace of black garnets was sent as a wedding present to my mother.

Time passed, circumstances and events intervened. Natalia Mihailovna learned of my birth—she kept in touch. After our departure to America, when all communication ceased, Papa made an effort to locate her through the Red Cross. He finally learned that after all her lands and holdings had been confiscated by the Bolsheviks, her former estate manager gave her refuge and cared for her lovingly in his humble home. She died shortly after this information was received. Through the years her name was revered in our home.

Very often, while wearing the unique black garnet necklace, which somehow survived and which I inherited, I would think warm thoughts of that elegant Edwardian lady, picturing her sometimes against the background of the estate that Papa described, and seeing her sometimes as she knelt laughing in the flower conservatory in front of my kneeling father—

"No! Neither will I get up until you retract your words!"

# MORE OF PAPA

The province of Volynsk or the fabled area of Volyn, from which Papa came, was scenic and rich in history. It boasted spreads of fertile agricultural soil in a northern region of the ancient Ukraine, and had high mountains to the southwest. Names of towns known to Russians in song and story abounded here—Zhitomir, Krementz, Roven, just to mention a few. The Kingdom of Poland once reached its arms into the region, flexing muscles, and lands passed back and forth between kings and emissaries like pawns on a chessboard. Legends wove themselves into the fabric of Russian tapestries and fired the imagination of poets and storytellers. Artist captured some of its beauty on canvases and composers paid homage to its splendor with operas and symphonies.

Papa loved the Volyn as a youngster, and became even more appreciative of it as a young man. He explored its areas whenever possible, listened to its legends, and as he said, could never get enough of it. There was never enough time, and he was curious about places where many historical events had taken place.

Thus he considered it a great good fortune when homeward bound from his military school in Odessa, he was requested to deliver a dispatch to an outlying estate near the province border. He had heard of the place, but had never seen it. Travelling in a hired carriage, he tried to recall what historical facts he remembered about the Mnishek Castle, as it was called. Its history related to the sixteenth-century rule of Ivan the Terrible, during which period a young upstart whose identity was never really established, proclaimed himself the true heir to the Russian throne, and became known to posterity as the pretender False Dimitri, claiming to be the slain son of the dead tsar. Gaining the support of the oppressed multitude, then of the militant Cossacks, and finally of the ambitious and assertive Polish lords, he obtained enough power to mount the throne and hold it briefly. His moment of glory was followed by his assassination and then two more similar similar pretenders who eventually met the same fate. However, in the beginning, when his star was ascending, he gained the favor and patronage of a powerful Polish nobleman named Mnishek and stopped at his castle to gather forces. Mnishek had a daughter Marina, a proud and ambitious beauty. Dimitry fell in love with her, promised her the throne of Russia as his Tsaritsa, wooed her ardently and managed to marry her. Eleven months later he was slain. Marina sought the protection of the second ill-fated pretender and ended her day in prison. Her only son, fathered by the first False Dimitri was hanged as a youth.

When Papa traveled to the Mnishek Castle, it was owned by another polish family and it was on Russian soil, not Ukrainian. Yet legends still clung to it, and Moussorgsky had written an entire opera "Boris Godunov" about the history of that period. The second act of the opera takes place in the castle. Feodor Chliapin, the great Russian "basso profundo," had made Boris his title role, and the opera, Moussorgsky's masterpiece, was based on an epic poem by the Russian poet Pushkin.

Papa had a special ability of describing people, scenery and situations. Listening to him I could easily visualize his impressions and relive his emotions. He spoke simply and directly, bringing up an exact image of the past, and I could see his beloved countryside and follow his carriage as it approached the walls of the Castle Mnishek.

After identifying himself to the gate-keeper, Papa left the carriage outside and was ushered into the courtyard. It was not a very large area. The castle being rugged and fortress-like, but on both sides of the entrance to the main structure there were two colossal porcelain figures of seated mandarins. Dressed in full Oriental ceremonial robes lavishly decorated, they sat with folded hands and benevolent porcelain smiles, guarding the massive doorway. And as Papa approached, some treadle installed in the cobblestones set off a mechanism which made the two giants slowly nod their porcelain heads and roll their eyes in their sockets. The unexpected effect was traumatic!

"It froze my blood a bit," Papa confessed, and it also froze; mine a little as I followed his story.

"Utterly, utterly fantastic—unbelievable!—tall as a good-sided house—all of porcelain, mind you—and nodding—and rolling their eyes!"

I could see it all.—A young man in uniform facing two grotesque Oriental giants in the middle of a sunlit courtyard. Some servants appeared, led him in, and he presented his credentials to the major domo. The master was away, would return shortly, but there was the daughter of the family to greet him.

"Yes—the daughter turned out to be a very lovely young woman. Played the hostess, was most gracious, asked me to wait her father's return and entertained me prettily."

"How exactly prettily?"

"Well,—first with a zakuski at a well-laden table, and then by answering my questions about the castle. Finally she took me on a tour and showed me things preserved from the days of the Mnisheks—the great hall, the armory, and the gardens beyond the castle. There she showed me the most famous spot of all—a crumbling stone seat in the shade of old trees. Here, she told me, Marina Mnishek and the False Dimitri plighted their troth. Naturally, we sat down."

"Did Marina sit where you were sitting?" I asked him.

"Possibly!—So we flirted a little and eventually returned to the castle to find her father and an arrogant-looking young man who was introduced as her fiance."

"You spoiled the ending," I said, deflated. But the charm of his tale remained with me. Years later, when I saw the opera "Boris Godunov," the garden scene with Marina and Dimitri was somehow more poignant and significant.

# AND A LITTLE MORE OF PAPA

Looking back on Omsk, on Semipaltinsk, the image of my father remains the same—a dedicated and courageous young man. Having fought valiantly in World War I, he was ready to tackle the Revolution, but underestimated its malignant force. Of middle height, slender, with brown eyes and features more delicate than pronounced, he had an unmistakable military carriage and a certain elegance in his gestures. Sensitive and idealistic, he also recognized reality and was a keen observer of the world around him. It is this trait of observation that I inherited more than any other—an ability to isolate oneself completely in order to view and study the passing scene. He had, however, many fast friends among his seminary classmates and then among his fellow officers. The letters from his soldiers in the front lines of World War I to my mother, testified that there was affection and esteem for their leader.

In his activities during World War I there was a strong bond of comradeship between him and the soldiers he commanded. He carried in the heart-pocket of his uniform a curious little wooden icon given to him by the Archbishop Anthony, whose altar-boy he had been in earlier years. It was blessed by the Archbishop with a "strong blessing," and how the knowledge of its power got around the camp remained a mystery. What is known, however, was the fact that often before a battle some soldier would waylay Papa and would have to do no more than mutter—

"Please, you excellency—the blessing—

Out would come the little icon from Pap's uniform pocket. He would make a sign of the cross over the man and let him kiss the icon. It was not more than four by six inches, painted on wood and depicted some saints and a worded prayer, yet it was instrumental in saving my father's life when he was wounded by deflecting a bullet. Years later it was buried with him.

Archbishop Anthony was a most colorful and powerful figure of a church man in his time. Outspoken, aggressive, entirely fearless, he was fiercely protective of his church and his tsar, yet he was also sophisticated and worldly. Auburn-haired and handsome he implemented his good looks by choosing vestments to set off his coloring—rich blues and turquoise brocades—and must have been a spectacular sight officiating in the great glittering cathedrals.

One of the duties of the altar-boy was to present on a kind of a platter the vestments which the Archbishop would don; a particular ritual of the service, performed with the Archbishop standing on a dais and consecrating each part of the vestments as they were offered to him. Being by that time entirely devoted to Anthony (whose namesake he was) Papa would spend most of his pocket money on some cologne or perfume with which he would sprinkle the garments generously beforehand. The fragrances of lilac, or rose, or lily-of-the-valley wafted their various scents to the sensitive nostrils of the Archbishop as he officiated, and Papa would stand with downcast eyes and innocent countenance, and hear, as each vestment was donned—

"Stinks like a wet dog!—you young ruffian—wait till I get my hands on you!"

All this in a threatening whisper between chants and supplications.

Later, side by side with the Archbishop in his carriage, Papa would receive a playful punch on the chin and a long-winded chastisement which usually ended with the recollection of the Archbishops own boyhood pranks.

Archbishop Anthony maintained contact with Papa throught he years. He sent his blessing when Papa was married, sent a very special one when Papa went to war, and when he was recuperating from his wounds in a military hospital, His Grace made a trip to visit him.

"He came brushing aside all welcoming ceremonies," Pap tells, "Came straight to my bed and took my face in his hands. 'Antosha, Antosha,' he said, calling me by his pet name, 'why didn't you have the sense to duck?'"

When I was born Papa asked him to be my Godfather, but his church rank prevented him from officiating in that capacity.

"I will be your daughter's spiritual Godfather," he replied and sent with his blessing the exquisite old icon which has been with me all my life. (My own grandmother and the commander of my father's regiment were my official godparents, but above them was the blessing of the Archbishop Anthony.)

There is a photograph of him in the family album, and a note stating that two crosses were being sent to the two "warrior brothers" (my father and his younger brother Ivan) with prayers for their safety. In the photo the Archbishop's gaze is concerned—his eyes seem a little troubled. We never learned what became of him, as he never left Russia.

I am not of the generation that writes "Mummy Dearest" confessions, or, like Rossevelt's son exposes his father's extra-marital affairs. My parents were normal human beings who made human errors in their lifetime, and it is not my purpose to demean them for whatever failings or to imbue them with impossible virtues. I am merely recapturing that which surfaces from that long ago period. Through the years that I spent with my father his reminiscences went back and forth—one day he spoke of Kolodno, next day of his duties in Omsk. The fragmented recollections sometimes come unbidden and sometimes elude me when I pursue them. It was only yesterday, and yet that yesterday was another age and another world.

But back to Papa. The training of cadet-ensigns in Omsk and Semipalatinsk was a task into which he put his heard and soul. He made it his business to know every individual under his care. He was also most exacting in choosing the assisting instructor-officers and following the progress of instruction. Remembering his own training he sought to maintain a program in which the latest technology and military tactics had a prominent part. And he was never happier than when surrounded by young cadets, among which group he was popular and respected. One of them, with an artistic talent documented some events in a sketchbook and presented it to Papa on graduation. I dimly remember something about that sketchbook. There was one drawing of a group of cadets standing stiffly at attention before a church altar blazing with candles. That was one of Papa's favorite drawings, and he recalls the incident.

"The whole class was stupid about something—I cannot recall just what it was—and after my patience was exhausted I felt justified to impose some form of punishment.—I sent them to the; military chapel to stand at attention for an hour and reflect upon their shortcomings. When the hour was almost up I went to the chapel to dismiss them. I found the building ablaze with light.—Every chandelier and candelabra glowed with candles, while the young men stood stiffly at attention. Before going in, everyone of them had bought candles and lit up the place like a bonfire!"

"And what did you do?" I asked.

"Dismissed them, naturally, but I also told them they were 'molodtsy'—which indeed they were!" ("molodtsy" was a term of praise meaning "great guys" or "splendid fellows!")

Graduating as officers and being commissioned to various regiments and posts, the young men always paid an official visit to my parents before leaving. Mama said it was unforgettable and touching how they come to the house in new officer' uniforms, always bearing a bouquet of flowers for her, and accepted a glass of wine from Papa on the basis of new equality. They parted with unashamed tears in their eyes, and the brown eyes of their chief commander would also mist over as he watched them go forth into an uncertain future. They were his pride, and they were so young and eager to serve.

Of exceptional value to him was one of their parting gifts—a silver cigarette case incrusted with gold and bearing a gold scroll engraved with some thirty names of the graduates. By some good fortune it was included among the things that came with my parents to America. A few interesting documents have survived. How they survived is described in the portions of this book pertaining to our flight toward Vladivostok. One of the documents is the curious and rare Imperial Edict, bestowing the Order of St. Stanislav and promoting Papa to the rank of captain "for excellent and decated service." These edicts, greatly valued and honored, began—"By the Grace of God, We, Nicholas the Second, Emperor and Protector of All Russias __" and went on with titles of the Tsar and the gist of the matter. The promotion to colonel came when edicts were no longer used even though the White Army was still in power.

There is also a document of his military service and a resolution of the Revolutionary Tribunal pertaining to his arrest and sentencing—events which did not come to pass because he escaped almost at once and went on to organize another coup against the Bolsheviks. Of these periods I cannot give details because I was too young to understand what went on, and I can recall only the incidents where I was directly involved. Even in later years when there were discussions of the revolutionary upheavals, the events seemed confusing and complicated. I do know that Papa and his detachments risked their lives several times in trying to stem the tide. I also know that when the Imperial Family was held captive in Ekaterinburg there was a plan to stage a rescue.—A plan which never materialized and the collapse of which haunted my father for the rest of his life. Although he was always willing to talk about World War I and the disintegration of a great empire, I think it pained him to speak of some of the facets of the Bolsheviks' terrorist regime.

That was Papa—Colonel Anthony Vsilievich Seletzky—a dedicated soldier and a man of high principles. He rests today a sea and a continent from his native land, but he rests in consecrated soil and the place is marked, honoring his memory and his name.

# MAMA—AND HER
# RECOLLECTIONS

When my mother was very young, her mother had borne a son who did not live long. My mother was attending the "gymnasia" at that time and delighted in making little bibs for the newborn baby brother. He was christened "Christopher" and they called him Kotik. When he died in infancy, she went to school on schedule and wondered why "the sun shone on as before" while there was such tragedy at home. Her homeroom teacher, learning of this later, commented on the fact that "young Alexandra was very quiet and remote, and did not tell anyone of the family's loss.

She was devoted to her school—her "gymnasia." The girls wore high-necked brown uniforms with a black apron for week-days and white aprons for holidays. In the anteroom of the school there was a uniform on a model so that exact copies could be made. Grandmother, handy with her needle, made the first uniform for Mama but put an extra tuck into the apron.—That was remarked upon, and had to be remedied. Instead of seven tucks, there had to be six.

There were tales and tales of the "gymnasia" where Mama spent seven years, all in the same classroom, always with the same classmates and the same "class-dame" who was in charge for severn years. What friendships were formed!—What developments took place!—To be for seven years with the same young people under the guidance of one woman would be incredible by today's standards!

They had classes in religion, Russian grammar and literature, French, German, science, mathematics, history, geography, art, music and dancing.

All in all, she must have had a rich and happy childhood and adolescence, amidst a family of a younger brother and older sister. There were loving grandparents also, maternal grandfather being the mayor of "X" where mother went for visits during summer vacations.

She says she had a pet kitten that she took with her on those visits in a little closed basket. The grandparents were most indulgent and went along with all whims. The kitten always disappeared when it was time to go home, and the entire household was engage in search while the carriage waited to take her to the train.

"My grandmother, your great-grandmother," she told me, "was married for the second time to the Mayor of the city and they lived in a very large house. In early years Grandmother had been a beauty and they talked about her in the surrounding counties. When she was sixteen, she was taken to visit some very wealthy neighboring landowners,. During the visit, a beautiful boy of about ten years, dressed in a velvet suit with a lace collar, came in to pay respects to the guests. He was the heir to the family fortunes, and Grandmother was impressed with his looks and manners. Years later that same boy became her second husband.

Several relatives lived with Mama's grandparents in their large house. One of them, Aunt Marcella, was devoted to Mama. She was somewhat withdrawn, not in the best of health, but full of imagination and love for young people. She and Mama were very close. As Mama grew to adolescence, Aunt Marcella took an interest in all that concerned her. She wanted Mama to be beautiful and disclosed a number of lod "beauty secrets"—like washing the face daily in milk, brushing hair with a brush wrapped in silk, bleaching the skin with cucumber, etc. These rituals were always performed during Mama's summer visits.

Mama was a mischief-maker—she had the run of the whole estate, and the grandparents were most indulgent. She would climb the back garden wall, which stood along a narrow street, and sprinkle the passers-by with water from a watering can. Someone, of course, would eventually complain, but heads were shaken, admonishing fingers wagged, and no punishment would ensue.

Another time, she told me, during a dsedate walk with both grandparents, she, for no reason at all ran ahead and butted her head into the protruding stomach of a very pregnant lady walking toward her.

"But why?—Why?" I demanded. "Whatever possessed you?"

"God only knows—she was so very big!"

The summer visits to the grandparents must have given her many happy days. She also had a good childhood at home. The "gymnasia" days were days of learning and friendships, and important associations.

She remembered her teachers.—The music-master who came every week and taught them many songs—a stern but just director—the "class dame" who was always there to solve problems and moderate—her friends and classmates. She loved to talk about them all.

The science instructor was a handsome gentleman and all the girls were in love with him. He charmed them with his experiments. "Bring me a scrap of silk," he said before the next experiment on electricity, and Mama came forth with some two yards of scarlet ribbon. During one experiment, while leaning over to watch, one young girl was so overcome by her infatuation, that she pushed forward and planed an impulsive kiss on the instructor's nape. They all gasped at her audacity, but the instructor brushed off the kiss with an indifferent gesture and went on with the experiment. She says that after class they mobbed and almost killed the girl, but of course the "class-dame" intervened.

The instructor of religion was an elderly, benevolent and a very wise priest. In upper classes he counselled them—"If life should ever place you in adverse circumstances, try never to live in a basement—choose an attic if you must—it will be a healthier environment spiritually and physically."

The "gymnasia" girls came from affluent families, from middle-class families, and a few were very poor and on special scholarships. They formed close friendships and were treated equally and fairly, as far as she could remember. There were some Jewish girls, and Mama had close friendships with them. Her friends were welcome in her home and she visited many. One of the photos shows her as a girl of about eleven or twelve with one of her young Jewish friends.

As she grew up, acquaintances broadened. Zhitomir had a clerical seminary and a university. Young men and women met and friendships developed. The parents were strict, but allowed and encouraged social activities. Mama was interested in the theater, and there were amateur theatricals. Guest artists coming into town for operas and plays found their way into many family homes and sometimes directed amateur performance.

Mama's parents had a large circle of friends. Her father, the Danish-born Georgy Kappel, was Post-master General in the town and held other civic offices. Among their friends was a very large and affluent family that was particularly close. Their name, of German origin, was Reihart, and the mother of the family, Maria Oskarovna, was a very beautiful worldly woman whose home was always open to friends, and who entertained on a lavish scale. There were many small children and teenagers. They were all devoted to the arts—music and theater—and stage many amateur performances in which Mama took part. The head of the Reihart family was devoted to Mama's father and frequently played violin duets with him. Mama's father, my own grandfather, was a great music lover who played the violin admirably.

One summer, during vacation, the enterprising young people stages a performance of "Eugene Onegin," directed by some theatrical friend. Mama had the part of Olga. The performance went off well, but after it was over, the entire cast, still in their costumes, made their way through the streets to the monument of the poet Alexander Pushkin, which stood in the city square. There they humbly begged his pardon for taking liberties with his masterpiece!

During school months visits to the theater were permitted only by special requests, both at the "gymnasia" and at other schools. In the theatre, a seat was reserved every performance for a "class dame" or an inspector, to insure that no student appeared in the audience without a special permit. The seminary students and other young male scholars often broke this rule by getting out of their uniforms and donning various disguises. On one occasion, while leaving the theater with a group of friends (all with legitimate permits), Mama was astounded to be familiarly hailed by a huge coachman who stood outside. After a momentary shock, she recognized him as one of the law students who frequented the Reihart Household. Dressed in the borrowed garb of a coachman, and brandishing the traditional whip, he had been aprt of the audience in the gallery, where the camouflaged students sought to escape the notice of their mentors.

Toward the end of school days there was naturally more freedom and more social activities. A grand masquerade ball was given by some exclusive club and Mama attended dressed as a Christmas tree.

"A Christmas tree!" I exploded. "What kind of a costume was that?

"Very attractive and striking. Your grandmother made me a dark green gown to which fir branches were attached. On those branches we fastened ornaments and typical decorations. I wore a large star on my head and brown satin slippers. There was also a star, which somehow got fastened over my thigh—" she hesitated.

"So?" I prompted, "a star over your thigh?"

"Well, that star—we all wore masks, you know, and it was customary in a masquerade to approach anyone and to address him with a familiar 'thou'—the masquerade had its laxity of rules. So, there was an elderly general standing by the wall watching the dancers. He was unmasked, as all officers were, but in his dress uniform with all regalia and a huge military star on his breast—well—I ran up to him and said, 'Sir, your star is in a wrong place.' He laughed and shook his head." 'Where should it be, my pretty?' 'Here' I said slapping my thigh and indicating my own tinsel star."

It was learned, a day later that Mama's father met the general at some public function. The man was visiting the city and had been invited to the club to view the masquerade. He told Grandfather he enjoyed it thoroughly and laughingly recalled that some "young minx dressed as a Christmas tree told him his star (the Order of Stanislaus?) was in the wrong place. Grandfather did not reveal that the "young minx" was his daughter.

"Were you scolded?" I asked.

"What for? Your grandfather thought it was rather a joke."

"I thought he was strict with you?"

"Everything had its place and time."

Through the years I thought of that incident many times. I vividly pictured a slim young girl in her bizarre costume pirouetting before the elderly dignified gentleman and teasing him about what must have been a very prestigious decoration on his uniform. He must have really enjoyed her youthful audacity.

She had many friends and must have been very popular. In later years there were several admirers. She speaks of one of them, a law student, Leonid Jerebko, who was quite devoted and even proposed to her. She learned much later that he died of consumption in middle age.

Then there were some stories of a third or fourth cousin called Koko who lived in st. Petersburg and visited infrequently. He was something of a fop, and his affected speech and mannerisms were a source of much amusement. "He spoke with a St. Petersburg drawl," Mama recalls, "a very aristocratic young man." He could not get over the ract that on the outskirts of the town household hens get would often roost on trees, and thought it was "remarkable." Probably the only hens he ever saw in his St. Petersburg appeared well browned and turssed on his mother's table.

When I look deep into my mother's recollections, I visualize an entirely different world.—A home presided over by a competent, understanding and loving matriarch, a cook in the kitchen, a couple of maids, a yard man, called a "dvornik," and a host of hirelings. There was a "vodovoz," a water carrier to bring in fresh water every day, a chimneysweep, "troubochist," a fresh produce man, a dairy man, etc. etc. There was also a seamstress who came in to help, a laundress, and many people with different services. Yet it was not a home of great wealth or affluence. Grandmother might have kept her two daughters out of the kitchen, but she did not discourage handwork or crafts. Mama began her exquisite needlework early. In the "gymnasia' they were fortunate to have an instructor who was talented and creative, and who gave freely of her knowledge. In the upper classes Mama was a star pupil in embroidery and fancywork. Using a very fine silk mesh, which was found only in sieves for fine pastry making, she embroidered with minute, bead-like cross-stitch a spray of flowers. It was set into a red plush square lined with red satin and studded with pearls. The whole thing became a most elaborate handkerchief case. She inteded to present it to her father as a birthday gift, a wonderful receptacle for his fine hand-monogrammed lined handkerchiefs. She worked on it very diligently, and, as it neared completion, complained at home that her eyes were suffering from the strain. The annual "gymnasia's" bazaar was being planned at the time, proceeds going to scholarship funds for the students who could not afford tuition. Many pieces of handwork were donated by girls from th e needlework class and although the instructor knew that Mama's handkerchief case was intended as a birthday gift, she persuaded Mama to donate it to the bazaar, as it was sure to sell for an impressive sum. Mama consented, and told the family about it at home, confessing that it was to have been a birthday gift.

"I will make you another one just like it," she promised her father.

"Never," he stormed. "I will not have you ruining your eyes on such a piece again. Go tell your teacher to put a 'sold' lablel on it, fix a fancy price and display it at the bazaar. I shall buy it."

And so he did. And the sachet still remains in my box with Mama's other work. It is very Victorian, and very beautiful to me. She must have been about sixteen when she made.

The school bazaar brings up another incident—the raffle of a beautiful large doll dressed in the exact replica of the "gymnasia's" uniform. She had a secret name, and one ws to buy a ticket and try to guess the name in order to win her. She was displayed in the auditorium days before the event. There was much speculation. Mama came home reciting all possible names to the family. "Nina? Tatiana? Ekaterina? Looba? Oksana?"

"You'll never guess it," her father said finally. "They probably have dug up some impossible name for her—like Evpestimia, or something similar."

He proved to be entirely right. A young seminary student won the doll with one ticket. He guess that her name was—Evpestimia!

"Only a seminary student could think of that," laughed my grandfather later. "They have the names of allChristiamn martyrs on hand in their missals."

Grandmother had made an acquaintance of a young Italian woman whose husband came from Italy to set up a small photographic studio in town. Grandmother learned that the young woman came from a wealthy Italian family, was convent bred, and had eloped with the photographer who courted her previously against the family's wishes. They were married, and eventually found their way to Russia. The young woman helped her husband in his studio and also tried selling some bits of exquisite and unusual embroidery of her own making. It was learned that the convent where she spent many years was noted for its handwork and the nuns taught the girls the art of the most beautiful embroidery and lace making. Needless to say, Grandmother took the young woman under her wing, helped her in many ways, and learned a great deal from her. Mama also benefited by this friendship and was taught many unusual methods of embroidery. She learned how to make dollies typical of an Italian design that was popular in the 16th century. Mama tells that the young woman in eloping with her husband-to-be, took with her only a small, carved casket crammed with samples of her convent work. She was very beautiful, Mama remembers, and delighted in teaching different methods of needlework.

The love for handwork never diminished in Mama's lifetime. She made lovely things throughout her life except for the last two years. She sewed my dresses beautifully and her own were often admired. She loved to make children's clothes and to dress dolls. In later life she made and sold many dolls in period costumes. A period costume doll "Betsy Patterson" is now in the Maryland Historical Society Museum. Another copy of it remains with me.

It is impossible to list the various items of Mama's making. They include dresses, suits, coats, hats, lingerie, costumes, accessories, household linens, aprons, bibs, trousseau items, boudoir items, and on and on. Her hands were never still. She also loved to pass her skill on to others. Samples of her work show a great variety, a great skill and great patience.

From the things she made, I still have a lovely strawberry runner with napkins and a runner with napkins of Italian cut work. These were all made while she was young in Russia. My father was most appreciative and admiring of her work. I remember he traced and enlarged designs for her. While he was a strict critic when it came to dress—he had a great sense of fashion design—he was always enchanted by her handwork.

It was often said that I came by my art talent "honestly," for people claimed that Mama "painted with her needle."

# SIBERIA—LIFE IN OMSK

The places where we had once lived are of great interest to me now, and I find myself examining pre-Revolutionary maps where so many names have been changed. Mama had been indignant to learn that Tsarskoe Selo was changed to Pushkin. "Thank God they have named it after a great poet," she observed. "otherwise they might have called it Sovietgrad or Tovarishchgrad, or something similar."

The detailed history of Siberian towns is hard to come by now. Omsk, in west Siberia, became its administrative center sometime in the 1800th century. It industrialization, however, did not begin until after the Soviet regime, but it was a city of importance because of the Trans-Siberian Railroad.

To many Russians living in Russia proper, Siberia seemed like another world, a primitive wilderness with an extreme climate. From early seventeenth century it was used as a penal colony and a place of exile. Large-scale colonization and culture came in slowly. However, realization of its resources was filtering through and various expansions were taking place. It needed far-sighted and dependable administrators, men of integrity and high intellect.

When my father was appointed to the staff of the Military school in Omsk for the training of cadet-ensigns, some people regarded his appointment with misgivings. Yet it was the quality of his service in World War I and the leadership of the man himself which made him highly desirable for the post.

Leaving the familiar places of their early youth, parting with relatives and close friends, leaving also many possessions, which could not be transported, my parents traveled to a totally strange territory, unaware that even stranger territories awaited them in the future.

In Omsk I remember three places of residence. The first two were somewhat temporarily expedient as accommodations for newcomers were scarce. The first was a rented small house, rather primitive, having a tiny enclosed garden on our side and a large yard on the other shared by other houses. My father's valet, Nicholai, was with us at the time and doubled as a cook and house man, having quarters somewhere off the kitchen. I think I occupied a corner of the bedroom and played in the garden in good weather. My father's duties kept him extremely

41

busy and the first months of adjustment in Omsk must have been somewhat difficult. Mama occupied herself with needlework and sewing. She did complain a bit because needed materials were not obtainable in local stores. The parcels, which my grandmother frequently sent from Zhitomir, were therefore greatly appreciated.

There were many peddlers in and out of Omsk, usually Chinese, travelling on foot with great packs of wares on their backs. The wares were mostly small household items, but also materials for dresses and shirts. Silk pongee was particularly desirable, coming in different weights and sometimes in pastel shades. The peddler, if admitted, would squat down, open his pack, and unfurl bolts of lustrous material. The bargaining would then ensue. He would be very persuasive in mutilated singsong Russian. It was always a special treat to be present at these transactions and to see him measure off required lengths with a metal stick under Mama's watchful eye.

Sometimes the peddler carried a sack full of tricks, and those peddlers were called "focusniks"—magicians. They would not perform unless paid a few coins in advance, and usually a group of neighbors would engage one for the benefit of children. The performance was always held outside in the yard because the "focusniks" were reputed to be notorious thieves. A small rug was spread on the ground, and a curious array of shapeless objects would be placed upon it. Those things turned into impossibly bright flowers, wriggling dragons and the like. Sometimes a small idol was set to preside on one corner of the rug, and if some trick refused to materialize, the "focusnik" wuld strike him blows with a rod. All this was done to a jabber of Russian and Chinese, which delighted the children.

The tiny garden where I played had drawf apple trees, which bloomed profusely in the spring. There I also found and ate my first wild strawberry, and discovered small purple flowers like the ones that Mama embroidered on her personal linens. A teenage girl named Galia brought home a white and tan puppy who rapidly grew into an enormous St. Bernard and was called Romi. He was a good-natured loyal animal, tolerating all my games and escorting my mother and me to a nearby church where he waited outside until services were over. He remained with the house-owners when we moved to our second place of residence. However, he roamed the streets freely and we would have encounters. On each occasion he would recognize me and express his happiness with much barking and cavorting. It was amazing how he seemed to remember, and once, after a considerable period of time, as we were leaving Omsk for Semipalatinsk, he turned up at the railway depot and headed unhesitatingly for us, almost upsetting me in his joy. I recall that I was particularly grief-stricken that he could not come with us, and my distress must have added considerable worry to Mama who was already overburdened with problems.

The second residence in Omsk was with a family of a retired captain named Rounsky. There we had private quarters but took our meals in the large dining room with the rest. Morning tea was served to us in our rooms. The house was large, with a wide verandah overlooking a formal garden beyond which there was an orchard and an abandoned dovecote. The dovecote, with its gingerbread trim, made an excellent playhouse, although I was discouraged from using it too often because it was felt that sunshine and fresh air were healthier. Nevertheless, playing in the dovecote held a particular fascination—that of being isolated from everything and everyone, and indulging freely in flights of imagination. This early development of personal resources served me well throughout my life and sustained me in difficult periods.

The Rounsky house was handsomely furnished, had a formal salon with a grand piano frequently used by family members. Of them I recall the tall white-haired captain, his pleasant elderly wife, and two daughters by a previous marriage. One of them was named Kaleria and was very beautiful. Of our own quarters I can only recall the area where my playthings were kept and the area with the tea table. The windows fronted a tree-lined street, and sometimes I leaned out on the broad sill to watch the detachments of soldiers march past on their way tot he grounds of their maneuvers. Sometimes Papa rode his horse alongside of them, and sometimes the soldiers sang as they went by. I remember some of their marching songs.

'Raz!—dva! Gorie ne beda! (One—two! Grief is not a woe!)

Milaya horoshaya—ya liubliu tebia! (Dearest and darlingest, I love you so!)

The song that I liked best was "The song of the Hussars!:"

Upraising the dust of the streets,

Their firearms aflame in the sun,

To the tune of the gay trumpeteers,

The gallant Hussars had marched on!

And there was just beyond a raised curtain,

A pair of blue eyes held a smile,

And the gallants all knew that their stay here

Would certainly be worth their while!

The regiment's now at its lodging,
The moon to the night lends her grace,
And the gray commanders are not dreaming
Of what under their windows takes place.

'In the morning upraising the dust,
Their firearms aflame in the sun,
To the tune of the gay trumpeters
The gallant Hussars had moved on.

And there just beyond the raised curtain,
A pair of blue eyes followed long.
The vanishing makers of mischief
Who now marched away with a song.

And often in bleak autumn twilights
Their laughter now misted by tears.
The blue eyes would often remember
The song of the gay trumpeteers.

The Rounsky family was most friendly and hospitable. I understand that the beautiful Kaleria had a definite "yen" for Papa, but she and Mama were the best of friends, and in later years when it was disclosed to me that she had, in deed, entertained a great affection, she was always warmly remembered by my parents. The captain's wife was extremely kind, frequently bringing me little treats from the kitchen and finding some Victorian gowns and furbelows for me to dress up in. I remember Mama's laughter when I confronted her once in a black jet-trimmed blouse which reached to my ankles and a great plumed Merry Widow hat.

The gardens of the Rounsky house seemed to epitomize the gardens so often mentioned in Russian literature, and in reading the old romances I always visualize that one particular garden which it had been my privilege to know. It had the shaded walks, the lilacs and acacias and cheremoukha bushes, the willows and the birches and aspens, the secluded summerhouse called "besedka" (conversation place), and the formally designed beds of flowers. It was my delight to bury my face in great clumps of lilac, to gaze keep into the incredible beautfy of a great scarlet poppy, and to realize that the flame of nasturtiums proclaimed the coming of autumn. Nasturtiums, in Europe, had always been the harbingers of fall, last to bloom, like the asters. My favorite flower—then and now—was stock—"levkoi" in Russian—whose nostalgic inimitable fragrance always seemed to stir some fain regret or longing for something that was long ago and far away. Tall spikes of those pastel-colored flowers grew in one corner of the garden, and to me their perfume was pure enchantment. They are considered old-fashioned today, and are rarely found among other blooms, but whenever I come across them, I can never resist purchasing a few stalks.

The third dwelling place in Omsk I recall most vividly. The one-story build-ing stood on a quiet narrow street, opposite a small lumber-yard and then rows of similar houses. A narrow fenced palisade ran beneath the windows, and in the back the kitchen opened on a large yard, which other neighboring huses shared. One of the front rooms off the living-room was occupied by a young army wife who was pregnant at the time with her first child. Her name was Sofia Grig-orievna Herzog, and not having nearby relatives she clung to Mama and became a dear and close friend. Her officer husband was away on missions—most of the time she did not know his whereabouts—but very bravely and uncomplainingly she waited out her time while stitching small garments and doing beautiful nee-dlework. She entertained us with stories of her childhood in the Caucasus where she was born. She had a rich store of tales concerning that rugged and darkly-romantic area. She also had a gift for imbuing them with their true color. On long winter evenings, wrapped in a huge fleecy shawl, knitting needles clicking in busy hands, Sofia Grigorievna would spin her tales—

"There was a half-ruined castle not far from where we lived, standing dark against the sky with empty windows—" Immediately I could see it. In that castle, so the story went, a beautiful wife unfaithful to her warrior-husband, harbored a lover. The husband, learning of the betrayal, came home one day from his cam-paigns, and luring the wife and her paramour into the part of the castle that was under additional construction, had them immured in a space between two walls. Immured! Bricked up! == the horror of it stayed with me for days and nights. Immured forever between two walls—it was a most horrible revenge—I could not get over it.

"Oh, it was centuries ago," sofia Grigorievna continued blithely, but—" mak-ing big eyes at me—"whenever we would ride past the castle we would always try to peer into the windows—"

I don't know just when her baby boy was born—I must have been sent away tos tay with some friends at the time—but I recall that he was called "Shurik," and had a short life-span, dying the following year when I was away in the village of Evgaschino. There is a photo of Sofia Grigorievna and her baby, inscribed on the back to my mother, stating that "we are now half a year old." She is a pleasant-faced woman with short hair, the baby looks a bit startled. I don't know what happed later. I think she was eventually reunited with her husband, but she passed on into the shadows like so many others. Now she remains only a memory and a photograph.

In this house we had a succession of cooks who were also housekeepers. "All such good women," Mama recalls. "So honest and so very clean!" The first one, named Marousia, stands out particularly—a trim, handsome girl with some education who left after a short period to become a photographer's assistant. Mama hated to lose her, but encouraged her to "better" herself. From time to time Marousia would drop in for a visit to report her progress. The two cooks that followed were hardy countrywomen, good-natured and willing workers, but both totally illiterate. One was Nasha and after her came Marfa.

At that time I not only knew my alphabet which Mama had taught me, but astounded everyone by my ability to read all my children's books. I loved books and on occasions when I had to be left in care of one of the cooks, I would bring them out and "explain" the pictures and read aloud the text. I don't know how it came about, but first one woman and after her the other, learned the alphabet under my guidance and went on to decipher words syllable by syllable. In other words, I taught them to read!

"She began her teaching career very early," Mama used to laugh in later years, and liked to describe how she returned home from a visit one evening to find a real lesson going on in the kitchen. "—and Masha was actually reading from a book—reading aloud, mind you!"

All that comes back from the past very vividly—the primitive kind of a kitchen—the scrubbed wood surface of the table with a kerosene lamp on it—the buxom, middle-aged woman underlying words with a work-roughened finger and laboriously deciphering the text or some fairytale or jingle.

A well-known old Russian proverb states that "learning is light, ignorance is darkness." Many country people unable to read, referred to themselves as being "dark." It was a popular expression in those days. I don't know how much "light" my so-called instruction shed into the lives of those two women, but Papa always claimed that they left our household with a considerable degree of "education."

Revolutionary events affecting my father took place in our third dwelling and it was from that house that Papa took me to the village of Evgaschino, but that comes later.

# VIGNETTES OF OMSK

In Omsk there were some friends outside the military circle—for example, a husband and wife that I remember well. I don't know what civil post he held, but the husband was a great sportsman and hunted frequently. In their small but comfortable house an enormous bearskin complete with a ferocious head hung over one of the couches. A beautiful hunting dog of a prestigious pedigree was taught to leap and bark at it whenever the master gave a signal. This performance was enacted for my benefit whenever we visited. On another wall, over the glory of a Caucasian rug, were displayed jeweled daggers, knives nd old muskets. On the plate-rails around the room were excellent examples of the taxidermist's art—pheasants, owls and all kinds of wild foul and woodland animals. The hunter, whose last name was Lihachevsky, was a great entertainer and fond of children. He was a bustling chubby fellow with a cherubic face, which contrasted strangely with his statuesque and dignified wife. He enjoyed relating tales of his hunting adventures, giving imitations of birdcalls and describing the attributes of various denizens of the forest. He sometimes took down one of the stuffed birds from the plate-rail, and placing it on my lap would point out the markings. Also, in imitating some birdcall he would take up two silver teaspoons and strike and rub them together to reproduce the sounds. This was usually at the dinner table with his placid wife admonishing, "Dovol'no! (Enough!) Let the guests eat in peace!"

Lihachevsky was also proud of the fact that his dog would not eat any other jam except gooseberry, and demonstrated the fact by spreading spoonfuls of various jams on a plate and offering it to the dog at his side.

Although there were no children of my age in that house, I was always happy to visit there, being highly entertained. When Lihachevsky went hunting he sometimes brought a brace of ducks to my mother, and she made of them a delicious pate from the treasured recipes entrusted to her by his wife.

In the house adjoining ours there was a teenage boy who played a violin. He was much older, handsome and very reserved, but sometimes he condescended to pull me around the yard on my sled, and did build for me a small snow-hill for coasting. In his own house I often saw him framed by one of the windows as he

stood before a music stand sawing away on his violin. The sounds never penetrated the walls, so it was a mute performance, which somehow fascinated me. He
was always entirely absorbed in his music, never giving a sign that he was being
observed.

A very plump young girl in the last year of her gymnasia frequently visited
Mama to learn needlework. Her name was Nina and Mama found her very dili-
gent and creative. I recall that some Italian cut-work was in progress and she
labored over an elaborate design of a swan among water-lilies. Part of the design
had to be cut out, and she was devasted when somehow she made a wrong inci-
sion. Mama helped her to patch it, but Papa teased and said that now her swan
had no tail. Nina took his remarks so much to heart that she started on another
similar piece, completing it without any mishaps. I noticed even in those early
days that Mama had a way with young girls, daughters of her friends. They clus-
tered around her, vied for attention, showed her their poetry albums, teased her
to teach them needlework, and sough her advice in matters of fashion and adorn-
ment.

"Alexandra Grigorievna!—Alexandra Grigorievna!"—their sweet young voices
were always demanding her attention, and she was always gracious and patient
and generous with her time.

Insisting always on an immaculate and orderly house and proud that all her
servants were "exceptionally neat and clean," Mama was horrified on day when
Papa said that Marfa chewed tobacco.

"Not tobacco, Barinya," Marfa replied scornfully when questioned, "I
wouldn't put such filth in my mouth. This is 'sera'—good for teeth and health.
See?" and produced from her mouth a large wad of a gray gummy substance. It
was disclosed that 'sera,' a kind of chewing gum from some unknown gelatinous
plant was in popular use among the Siberians.

"Everybody chews it here in Siberia," Marfa went on to enlighten Mama. "It's
ever so good for the teeth, and it lasts and lasts forever, unless you forget where
you stuck it to give it a rest."

If some Siberian customs were somewhat hard to take, there was one that
delighted us all. Called to the front windows by one of the cooks, Mama and I
witnessed a cavalcade of sleds approaching. They, and the horses drawing them,
were garishly decorated with artificial flowoers, ribbons plumes and rosettes. On
each sled a group of young women in colorful holiday attire stood waving sheaves
of flowers and bunches of dried laurel, clapping vigorously and singing with
abandon to the accompaniment of accordions and balalaikas. Neighborhood
children and barking dogs racing and cavorting around complete the scene.

"They're taking the bride to the bania!" the cook explained to us.—A local custom of escorting the bride-elect to the public bathhouse just before the wedding by her bridesmaids. We were to witness these excursions many times during our stay in Omsk, and it was never possible to distinguish the bride from her colorful companions, because she waved gand clapped and sang with the same exhuberance. How well I remember somebody in the house calling, "Quick! Quick!—over to the windows!—The bride is riding to the bania!" and the noisy cavalcade streaking by, heaving an echo of merriment in its wake.

Another kind of; cavalcade frequently came down our street—the Khirgiz traders from the north. They rode in low-slung primitive-looking sleds drawn by dromedary camels who stepped disdainfully over the snowy road with dignity and nonchalance, indifferent to everything around. The drivers, whose Mongolian features could be glimpsed under their curious hats with long ear-flaps, sat in fur-lined overcoats and boots of thick felt. Piled around were the wares they brought in for trading, mostly furs, leather, dried fish and walrus ivory. They seemed as remote and indifferent as their animals—strange figures gliding by in a silent caravan against the background of snow-covered town houses. On closer observation some of the drivers might be found missing a nose—victims of intense frostbite in their regions.

When I think of Omsk I associate summer with the Rounsky house and garden, and winter with this third residence. I also bedame aware there of a distinct change of atmosphere, and aura of special alertness and apprehension. My father absented himself more frequently for days and nights, messengers came at all hours, Mama had many women visitors and looked abstracted most of the time. I heard her say once to Sofia Grigorievna—"our street is a very quiet one here—I don't expect any demonstrations—" and finding me nearby, abruptly sent me off to play. The surroundings looked the same, everything was in its place, but it was as if some unseen menacing force crouched beyond the façade of the wooden houses, and everyone was cognizant of its presence.

# THE DISQUIETUDE OF A QUIET CHILD

By nature I was a quiet child, keenly attuned to the sights and sounds about me. Never neglected, never unloved, and seldom lonely. I existed, nevertheless, in a solitary state, as sometimes happens with only one child in a family. My parents did not spoil me. They surrounded me with warm affection, but kept a watchful eye on my progress, expecting me to be a well-behaved and courteous as they themselves always were. They gave me credit where credit was due, and recognized my individuality without inflating my ego. From my pinnacle of present age, and whatever wisdom I have accumulated, I can see and understand now that both were rather unusual young people. Not of nobility, but gentry folk. Extremely well-born, their standards, moral values, understanding and compassion were sterling qualities in a world that was being gradually devastated by dramatic and tragic events.

If Papa sometimes jokingly spoke of me as his "heiress," my inclination was to be seriously worthy of the title, and as I was aware of his rank and esteem of his peers, I unconsciously strived to present my best self on occasions when I was in the midst of grown ups. I missed my grandmother's loving presence a great deal, but I was learning to depend upon myself more. My personal resources were developing early. I listened and absorbed and I looked and absorbed. Like a small wild creature of the forest guided by instinct alone, I sensed the climate of events even before they came to pass.

Subtle and insidious and disturbing is this felling of vague, vaporous apprehension. One first becomes aware of it in the looks which pass like messages between people, in the sudden cessation of conversations, in a certain new light, which illuminates familiar objects from a differnet angle. There is a kind of tension—simple actions become intense.

"Gospodi! Gospodi! Gospodi!" mutters the cook in the kitchen kneading the bread dough with more than her usual vigor.

"Everything is fine—just fine! Tomorrow we will go over to Lihachevsky's and you can play with the dog—" this from Mama who has been out all day and feels, somehow, that she has to reassure me and "make up" for something. There's a treat of special pancakes for supper, a visit to an officer's family across the street where there are young children and an old family nurse who can tell marvelous fairytales.—No time at all with my father who dashes in, envelopes me in a great bear-hug and is gone again. Mama does not say much, but makes a sign of the cross as the doors slam after my father. Outside it winter, the days are gray, the house has lost its coziness—evenings are long and dark, and always there is the rattle and knock at the doors, stomp of heavy boots—messengers from headquarters come and go.

Papa returned once totally exhausted from one of his mysterious trips, greeted us briefly, and pulling off his muddied boots went straight to the bedroom where he at once fell into a deep sleep. We went about on tiptoes, and Marfa prepared a meal in the kitchen. It was not long, however, before there was a knock on the front door and an officer came to fetch him, apologizing to Mama. They had a hard time waking him, and while he was getting dressed again in heavy winter garb, Marfa came in with a dish of something hot and savory.

I remember Papa emerging from the bedroom fully dressed, eyeing the streaming dish on the table, patting Marfa briefly on the shoulder as he passed, and disappearing into the cold darkness of the night with the man who came to fetch him. She stood over the untouched food shaking her head and saying to my mother—"And they don't even give him time to swallow something."

That kind country voice and the commiseration it carried, remains in my memory What happened, where are the Marfas, the Mashas, who were a part of our lives?

My vignettes of Papa now become different. Where he was sketched before with graceful strokes and studied shadings, the outlines now become more foreceful and abrupt. His entire personage may be captured in a few lines—the watchful eyes above the upturned collar of the uniform great coat—the alertness of the stance, like a coil ready to spring, the glimpse of ammunition in the strapped belts. No longer the polished, dandified gallant of the military, but the rough-rider of night, defender of the last vestiges of his civilization.

These are the few bare facts that I do know concerning him and the Bolshevik Government.—Recognizing his leadership and influence over his men, they wanted him to come over to their side, offering a prestigious position in their ranks. When he resisted, they placed him under house arrest and prepared for a trial that was to send him to years of imprisonment. Aided by detachments of loyal men and having gathered more opposing forces in his contra-revolutionary maneuvers, he escaped before the trial under their very noses.—Fled the house, fled Omsk, and to make it easy for my mother to hide—took me with him.

# THE ESCAPE TO THE
# VILLAGE OF EVGOSCHINO

"You will go travelling with Papa," Mama informed me cheerfully as she and Marfa packed some things. "I will come and join you a little later and we will have such a fine time."

"You will go travelling with your Papa," echoed Marfa—"and how lovely that will be—on a steamboat up the Irtusch, yet!"

I don't remember anything except Papa depositing me in a cabin of a steamship—a very small cabin that had a narrow bunk. He counseled me to be "a good, good girl!—get some sleep," and said we were going to "a very nice place." Very loving he was, and very harassed. He found a sympathetic young woman to minister to my wants, and of the journey I remember nothing until we disembarked in Evgoschino at dawn. Anxiety, irregular meals and the strangeness of the entire situation took their toll, and I was limp with nervous exhausttion and a little sick when Papa carried me ashore. Someone took over, undressed me, placed me in a soft and warm bed, and I fell into a deep sleep, which eventually did much to restore me.

The morning found me waking in a large lofty room with many windows. I was on a cot banked with pillows, and Papa was sleeping on the floor on a mattress nearby. We were, as I presently learned, in the home of Vasilisa Ivanovna. I do not recall her surname—an elderly widow of a prosperous Siberian merchant. She was a woman of influence in her area, and being fiercely protective of the "old regime" and mindful of her own considerable holdings, had given Papa and his counter-revolutionaries great support. Distrustful at first when he approached her concerning matters of headquarters, forest hide-aways and the like, she was soon completely won over and placed at his disposal not only that which he requested, but encouraged some of her village people to join his cause. She added horses and provisions and turned over a couple of barns for their use. She also assured him that both Mama and I would always find a safe harbor with her, and offered to take care of me until Mama joined us. I don't know just when Papa met Vasilisa Ivanovna—it must have been during his maneuvers over the countryside—but at the time of my arrival, she was in complete accord with him and urged him to go on with his missions, which he did at once, leaving me with her.

She represented the old order of wealthy Russian merchant families so often featured in literature, sometimes satirized, sometimes exaggerated, but always a colorful and important social group that commerce and manufacture produced. Without much formal education, she nevertheless had the highest regard for culture and learning. She had made the Grand Tour of Europe with her husband in earlier days. Now she shrewdly managed her estates, had her finger in every village pie, and operated a network of village espionage, which perhaps rivaled my father's military scouts in ability to ferret our necessary information. She was then in her late sixties, generously endowed, dignified and meticulous in her dress—the most prominent figure in the village. In the library of her elaborate home were gathered handsomely bound collections of all Russian classics, housed in glassed cabinets, and sad to say, unread by anyone. There were imported figurines and wax flowers under glass bells, mirrors and girandoles, rich carpets on the floors and a great deal of silver on the sideboards. Although the bania, the bathhouse, was in the courtyard as was customary, there was a "private closet" in the house with a commode upholstered in velvet. The house itself was, of course, the largest and teallest in the vilalge, being two stories high and boasting turrets, gables, and an elaborate fence with carved gates. Within the courty ard there was the bania, the stables, a barn, and a special fire-proof storage area. Evgoschino was considered a "progressive" village and there was electricity everywhere, even in the barns. Not far away was the harbor and landing areas for boats, barges and steamships that came and went. Birch and evergreen forests enclosed the village on two sides.

The kindness and good intent of Vasilisa Ivanovna eased my anxieties, and I began to feel secure in her presence. She had a cot brought into her own bedroom and placed alongside her immense four-poster. Never did she leave me alone during those first strange days. She sought to divert and amuse me, and I think my quiet demeanor worried her a bit.

"Who do you take after, Little One?" she would ask me, stroking my hair—"your Papa never stops whirling around and talking! Is your Mama quiet, too? Can you smile for me?"

It was not long before I not only smiled but laughed and ran about the house, following her from room to room, venturing out into the courtyard. Childless herself, she was a godmother to most of the village children, and was fond of pointing them out on our outings.

That's Tania over there—she's only nine but already she can knit stockings.—That one with the rabbit teeth is Petka—ohh, what a worthless scamp!—And here's the latest, little Vasilisa, named after me and christened just last week!"

The good woman had a retinue of village servants who congregated in her immense kitchen where she herself liked to spend considerable time supervising baking or making of preserves. She was a true "pomeshchitsa" (a wealthy landlady who managed her property). Her speech was full of old Russian proverbs, and she spoke to the villagers in their own broad dialect, reserving more "cultural" speech for more elevated individuals. I became attached to her and strove to please her. All this time my father was away, putting in an occasional brief appearance and then riding away again with two or three men in attendance.

"How's it going, Vasilisa Ivanovna?" he would ask her on arrival. "What do you hear?"

"Well, dorogoy moy (my dear)—the Evil is quiet, and the Good is not visible—that's how."

She fed him rich meals on his returns, and gave him the best quest-chamber if he stayed the night, although he protested that he could sleep on any couch.

"For whom shall I save the chambers?" she grumbled. "The tsar is not likely to visit an old woman out here!"

She was also impatient to meet Mama who was to arrive as soon as things "quieted down." It was the time of political checker-board games between the Bolsheviks and the counter-revolutionaries: a time of government disintergration, cross-purposes, murky intrigues and reversed directions. Admiral Kolchak" organization of anti-Bolshevik government in Siberia, although recognized by Russia's allies, was not without peril to the officers and soldiers loyal to the cause. The frequestnly mentioned names of ministers, military leaders and other officials were meaningless to me at the time. Under the care of Vasilisa Ivanovna I absorbed the sights of village life, went berrying with her into the neighboring forest, attended church, rode out into the fields and awaited Mama's arrival. The servants were also kind, and I particularly remember Efimovna who acted as housekeeper—a very old woman with a lined face and a thick braid of white hair wound around her head. She was known as a story-teller, and in the evenings she sat in the kitchen with her knitting and an ancient tom-cat draped around her shoulders. She related tall tales of village life where evil spirits were always featured, dead men sneezed in their caskets at their burial services, and young girls were dragged into the marshes by water sprites. Other servants gathered around her to hear, but Vasilisa Ivanovna disapproved of such stories, and finding me among the wide-eyed audience, took me away to the upstairs rooms where she would open a large carved music-box and allow me to choose and insert disks that played various airs. I must confess that Efimovna's tales fascinated me even though I scurried past darkened rooms and pulled the covers over my head at night. I really preferred the tales of "domovoy" (house-spirits) and the "rousalkas" (water nymphs) to the insipid tinkling of the music-box.

I was relaxed, not unhappy nd accepted most things without questions. So, when I was informed one early morning that a visit to another village was planned, I looked forward to the outing.

We had been in the havit of rising early, and the sun was coming up, promising a bright day. There seemed to be some haste in the departure, and breakfast was hurried. A carriage with a team of horses stood ready in the courtyard. Cushions and covers were piled high over the seats. Vasilisa Ivanovna, afflicted from time to time with gout, had not been well the past few days, and now had to recline fully in the crriage. I was packed in beside her, and we set off. The servants remained in a group behind, making signs of the cross after us as we rode out of the gates. I remember that we went through a dense forest of evergreens for most of the day. The driver, a stalwart bearded muzhik, long in the service of Vasilisa Ivanovna and accustomed to addressing her with the familiar "thou," drove steadily at a brisk pace, stopping only briefly a few times to rest the horses. The forest road was narrow, great trees closing in on both sides, so there was no scenery to watch. Vasilisa Ivanovna dozed. I was restless and tired. We had a meal of some kind from a basket with provisions. It was long after sunset and growing dark when we arrived at our destination. A room in some cottage was made ready for us. The pillows and coverlets transferred to a makeshift bed, and I fell asleep beside Vasilisa Ivanovna.

Next morning I learned we were in the cottage of the forester. His family shyly surroudned us and attended to our wants. The cottage—a typical "izba'—was primitive, but very clean, completely encircled by trees. It was completely isolated although a small village was located not far away. Vasilisa Ivanovna, not the worse for wear because of the tedious journey, continued to recline, but spoke to many people who came to greet her from the village.

I think we spent a week or more at that cottage, during which time I played with the forester's two timid children and ventured outside after I was assured that there were no bears or wolves in close proximity. "Although," said the forester's wife, "in winter the wolves do come right close, smelling our goat and horse."

Since only a dress had been packed for the hurried journey, I was in a sad state with little to wear. Finally the forester's wife offered a couple of garments belonging to her daughter who was my age. These coarse country clothes delighted me, and I preferred them to my own things. It was curious how I longed to assume the identity of a "true country girl," and imitated the little daughter of our hosts by sticking wild flowers in my braids and learning to plait crude wreaths from various grasses. I went barefoot, as did the children, kicking off my sandals, and Vasilisa Ivanovna, not being well, did not remonstrate.

Thus it was when Papa beheld the scene which became very dear to him over the years.—Barefoot, unkempt, with drooping blossoms in my hair, I was busily avoiding the advances of a great hissing goose when Papa and two attendants rode in from the density of the forest. He said that I almost dashed under the hooves of his horse when I saw him. He said that he swept me up with one arm. He had been looking for me and Vasilisa Ivanovna for three days, getting lost again and again before they found the remote village and were directed to the forester's home.

It never occurred to me to question why we had come there, but I learned after that Papa had been traced to Evgoschino by the Bolsheviks and that they knew he had taken his child there. Learning this from her own sources, Vasilisa Ivanovna ignored her indisposition and spriited me away. Papa, meanwhile, doing very well with his forces, arrived at Evgoschino to say that his missions were, for the time being successful, and found us gone. The servants were reluctant to disclose the place of our escape, and he had great difficulty in finding it.

"Like being in a green maze," he related. "Little forest paths leading to nowhere—I was seing nothing but green, green, green!—great menancing trees—then finally that primitive village—then, thank God!—an articulate fellow who pointed the way—"

What a reunion that was! How grateful he was for Vasilisa Ivanovna's care!

"Eh, dorogoy moy," she sighed snatching away her hands which he kissed over and over again. "For what should you thank me? I'm an old woman, and you and yours have a whole lifetime before you. Tell me now, what else could I do?"

We went back to Evgoschino with Papa and his men escorting the carriage through the forest. Once in a while Papa would lift me off the cushions and place me on horseback before him, holding me with one arm as the horse picked its way through the narrow rutted paths. Vasilisa Ivanovna dozed and relaxed in the carriage, feeling much better. A stronger force was now in charge.

Papa was gone again as soon as we reached our village, but a few days later a little steamboat with a hoarse foghorn brought Mama from Omsk. Vasilisa

Ivanovna opened her arms to her as if she had known her always. They became friends at once, and a kind of tranquility—perhaps a false one—permeated the next few weeks. The feeling of tension was gone. The summer in Evgoshino was a memorable one.

# THE EVGOSCHINO
# INTERLUDE

I was blissfully happy to be reunited with Mama in the home of Vasilisa Ivanovna. She had assured Mama that I had been a very good child indeed. Both she and Mama made much of me, as if to reward me in some way for some extraordinary behavior, but as I honestly felt that I had not put out any extra efforts, I wondered why they considered my conduct admirable. Did Vasilisa Ivanovna expect tears and tantrums when I was left with her? Did she expect a spoiled brat? I nev er indulged in any tantrums, and my tears, when I shed them were quiet and private. At any rate, I basked in their approval, and missing my grandmother, found some comfort in the person of Vasilisa Ivanovna.

She could not do enough for Mama, treated her as a beloved daughter, showed her all the house treasures, took her on rides visiting neighbors, introduced her to the landowners Kalishnikovs, and finally arranged a visit to her older sister in a village some miles away. That visit I remember.—A storybook country house within a richly flowering garden—an elderly lady greeting us on the entrance steps with a bouquet of flowers. In showing us the house she led us through delightful old-fashioned rooms, and in one there stood a high bureau on to of which was a little round mirror on a stand. Years and continents later my husband brought into our household a very similar little mirror on a stand, which he had made as a boy in a high school shop. I still have it, and I still wonder how similar designs originated in two different worlds.

With old Efimovna hobbling before us we went to gather blackberries and mushrooms in a nearby forest. She pointed them out with her gnarled walking stick.

"These ones—these you may pick aplenty!—they are the openki, so tasty in a pie.—And these little one are the grouzdki, good for drying and pickling. But God save you from touching these ones—" indicating a family group of bright spotted toadstools. They looked like the ones pictured in my storybooks, exactly like the ones Little Red Riding Hood passed as she hurried on her errand to her grandmother, exactly like the ones that Ivan Tsarevich went by as he rode on the back of his Gray Wolf. It is small wonder that the majestic Russian forests featured in the age-old fairytales inspired the writers and the artists. To enter them was to enter a world where anything was possible—enchantment, adventure and pure fantasy. In his prologue to the epic poem of Ruslan and Ludmilla," the poet Pushkin pays deep homage to the wonders of the forest, and among Russian artists, the landscape painter, Ivan Shishkin, was known as the "giant of the Russian forest." Dim, very dim is my actual memory of those pine groves and thickets, but much of the feeling has been retained. I am indeed fortunate to have had a glimpse of that grandeur with its dense masses of greens, its mystery of light and shade, the breathing and pulsating of its strange secret life.

"Ah-oo! Ah-oo!" someone's forest call echoed through the silent and yet not silent green gloom.

Ah-oo" I piped back, and old Efimovna noded approval.

We took walks down to the river tos ee the fisherman bring in their catch. Out in the courtyard of her home Vasilisa Ivanovna rolled up her sleeves, donned a voluminous apron, and began helping the cook clean the fish. The iridescent scales showered the flagstones in a silver spray and the army of household cats moved nearer and twitched with anticipation. Mama sat a little distance away embroidering something, and Papa, arriving unexpectedly in high good humor began to tease her for being "so-lily-handed" to join the fish cleaning.

Vasilisa Ivanovna rose to Mama's defense, told Papa to be off, and when he persisted, picked up a large fish, and swinging it adroitly, slapped him with it! Kissing the fishy hand that dealt the blow, Papa fled to the bania to wash off, leaving a hilarious group behind. That incident became a classic in our family, and Mama loved to relate it.

The fish pies and the mushroom pies and the berry pies that were baked were unlike anything I had ever tasted. The crusts, while, coarser, were more delectable. There were also many other old Russian dishes favored by Vasilisa Ivanovna, and now that she had house guests, she was entirely absorbed in culinary arts. I am sure that many of the dishes she served are now a legend, although some may still be in existence in parts of Russia.—The cold borscht made of kvass which Pap loved, another soup of fish called "ooha," still another favored by the peasants called "okroshka." Then there were rich pirogs with chicken and other fowl called "koorniks," roasts and mrinades of all kinds, pates of woodcock, duck and pheasant. For desserts there were "airy pie," charlottes, mousses, kissel, plombir and "zephyrs." Pirozhki were made with a variety of fillings, and always there was the "karavai"—the epitome of Russian hospitality when presented on a platter with a pinch or contained of salt to welcome honored guests. That ancient custom is still in favor in all levels of society. Many households have special platters of metal or wood for this purpose.

As though sensing that the sun was steadily setting upon her empire, Vawsilisa Ivanovna made most of every new day, entertaining frequently the Kalishnikovs and other neighboring landowners, proudly showing Mama off to them. Mama had become her special darling. And Mama, devining the older woman's need for family affection, responded with genuine warmth and appreciation. Used to the village children, Vasilisa Ivanovna was especially pleased with my behavior before her guests, and looked on with pride when I made my curtseys or took around the platter of sweets at her teas. From time to time she did call in some of her godchildren to play with me, but the children, coming in scrubbed and dressed in their best, were painfully shy of the "big house" and its chatelaine, and our game were stiff and not successful. Their responses to my overtures were slow, but once started they were eager to inform Mama and me of their own achievements. Tiny tow-headed Glasha said, with some pride, that her mamka (mother) was teaching her to milk their cow.

"And you're not afraid to do that?" Mama tried to help in drawing out the children.

"Niet, Barinya, our cow is very kind."

"My mamka lets me knead the bread dough!"

"Mine lets me feed the hens and get some eggs!"

"Mine is letting me sew some on Dounia's things. Our Dounia is getting married to Stefan next month—only we don't like Stefan because he swears too much—"

It was all very enlightening—I learned new words and expressions, not all of them acceptable to Mama, acquired a pair of birch-bark sandals plaited by someone's elder brother, and learned to treat mosquito bites with spit (which I do to this day). Also, to this day I swear by "Holy Friday" whenever it is necessary to assure someone of my intentions.

"Promise me to write—promise to come again soon!"

"I promise!—I swear by Holy Friday!"

My brush with nature's children, my glimpse of the soul of Russian peasantry—the pastoral scenes of my native land—these are rich experiences for which I am profoundly greateful, and even above that, I am grateful for the memory which retained and held them until I could put it all down in writing.

There was one traumatic event toward the end of summer—a great fire in the village. Many dwelling, barns and granaries were destroyed. It happened at night when everything is more menacing and dramatic. Awakened and quickly dressed by Mama we watched the sinister glow light up the sky and the leaping flames beyond buildings not too far away. In Vasilisa Ivanovna's courtyard there was much activity—she had the fireproof closet opened and servants carried into it some of her prized possessions. People who fled from burning homes found refuge with her, and she and Mama were busy administering to frightened people until dawn. I was placed in Efimovna's care, and the old woman gathered me with other children around her and kept us calm, comforting the crying ones and praising others for being "good."

By morning it was learned that the fire was a great calamaity. Arson was strongly suspected—Vasilisa Ivanovna was not without her political opponents. Many people were homeless and sought shelter with friends and neighbors. A wife of a military courier under my father's command had also been residing in the village for the summer. She had two children—a girl my age and an older boy who was a hunchback. They came to Vasilisa Ivanovna in their night clothes, as their cottage burst into flames without warning, and the mother, seizing a valise with some valuables and documents, dragged her children out and made way straight to the "big house." All their possessions were gone, but they were given quarters, clothes, and Vasilisa Ivanovna housed them until the husband returned with Papa to take charge. I remember those children—the memory of the girl is dim, but the brother's image is clear—a bright, cheerful little fellow unmindful of his back. We played together and looked a picture books in the library room. Mama set to sewing dresses for the ittle girl with the materials that Valilisa Ivanovna supplied, and everyone strived to make them as secure and comfortable as possible. No lives were lost in the fire, and the following Sunday Vasilisa Ivanovna requested a service of thanksgiving in chruch after which the entire congregation trouped to her home for a repast which was served on trestle tables in the courtyard. Many people came to kiss her hand and thank her for aiding them. The church choir lined up and sang "Mnogie Leta" (Many years). That particular refrain is a joyous one, just as its opposite, "Vechnya Pamiat;" (Eternal Memory) sung at burials, is a mournful one. Yet I can never hear either one without tears.

And so the choir sang to Vasilisa Ivanovna __

"God grant her many years!
God grant her many years!
God grant her many—many years!"

# THE LANDOWNERS
# KALISHNIKOVS IN
# EVGOSCHINO

The Kalishnikov family members were close friends of the merchant's widow with whom I stayed in the village of Evgoschino. They were wealthy landowners of estates and farmlands. There was Nicholai Aleksandrovich Kalishnikov and his widowed sister. I do not remember the late husband's status, but he had been of some importance in the government. Brother and sister were in their forties, handsome, aristocratic, hospitable and worldly. They lived in a large; manor house surrounded by many smaller building. There was an outlying park of considerable size. The sister had lavish apartments in the manor and acted as official hostess since her brother was a bachelor. Her name was Natalia Aleksandrovna Kalishnikova. She was dark-eyed and slender and totally devoted to her brother.

Nicholai Aleksandrovich was well-educated, well-traveled, a true bon-vivant, compassionate and elegant. He was well thought of by his people, and intelligent in matters pertaining to his lands, which he loved with all his heart and soul. It was no secret that he had a mistress installed in a separate house on the estate. She was a very beautiful young woman who had been a circus bareback rider. She had a luxurious little house and was treated with every courtesy, making appearances in the family circle only when there were close friends present. Otherwise she lived in isolation. My mother and Natalia Aleksandrovna became friends and family circumstances were soon disclosed. The mistress of Nicholai Aleksandrovich was introduced.

I dimly remember a very lovely shy person who took me to her little house and showed me her magnificent collection of dolls. She must have been a very lonely individual for she took such delight in showing me her beautiful things. Even then I seemed to be aware of the tragedy of this young woman who spent her days in the shadow of the "big house," surrounded by every luxury, but still so very much alone. There was no questions of marriage—she was there temporarily, to be loved and cherished by the master for a time, then to be sent away, well provided for when he choose to marry "quality."

I wondered about her a great deal, some overheard adult comments penetrating my understanding. She gladly played with me, and allowed me to handle her dolls. We dressed and undressed them, trying on beautiful miniature garments that came from France in miniature trunks. There were lacy pegnoirs, sumptuous ball gowns, fur-trimmed cloaks, plumed hats, muffs, fans, parasols, and handbags. The dolls had beds, scaled down furniture, porcelain tea sets and caskets of miniature jewelry. I remember sitting among this incredible collection, stroking reverently the ostrich plumes of some velvet hat, arranging the folds of a taffeta gown, yet feeling no envy at sll for all those fabulous toys. There was something pathetic about it all, which I felt even as young as I was. Later, one of the maids would come to escort me to the "big house" where Mama and Natalia Aleksandrovna were visiting together.

Natalia Alexandrovna observed everything with dark brown velvety eyes, lifting a finger here and there, never lifting her voice. In her luxurious boudoir, over cups of tea, she conversed with Mama while I sat on a ittle velvet footstool with a plate of sweer cakes on my lap. I admired the slippered feet our hostess—the satin slippers had tiny ermine heads with beady eyes, and they fascinated me. From time to time she and Mama would glance at me—"

"So, little one—is everything as you like it?

"Thank you, Natalia Aleksandrovna—I like very much your slippers."—and I reached over to stroke the little ermine heads while she and Mama laughed.

There were several large barn-like building around the manor. One of them was called "The Sweet Barn," and held sweets and imports needed for desserts. From it came the little gifts for me—chocolate "bombes," which were hollow balls of chocolate containing a "surprise" in the form of a tiny porcelain figurine of a filigree trinket. A chocolate "bombe" from the "Sweet Barn" was a very great treat, and I treasured the "surprises." I remember that one of them was a tiny porcelain figurine of a red fox.

There is one particular memory forever associated with that summer. Mama and I were invited by Nicholai Aleksandrovich to ride out and see the harvesting of one of his wheat fields. Now, the golden harvest days have been celebrated in songs and poems and stories and have been immortalized by masters on canvases.—There were endless fields where stalks of golden grain rose and fell as they rolled in waves with the wind; above skylarks soared heavenward leaving an echo of their song to haunt the hearts of the men who where under the hot, blazing sun. Their powerful figures bent rhythmically as they harvested the bounty and tied it into sheaves. It was like that, and I was privileged to glimpse it in all its primitive splendor.

We rode out to the fields in a light carriage with Nicholai Aleksandrovich driving. We arrived at a field where harvesting was taking place. It was such an expanse of gold—and—blue,—beauty as to leave one breathless: the enormous dome of the sky—the vast fields of golden grain—the blaze of the yellow sun—the smells of the earth and wheat—and the classical stance of the harvesters. It was a scene from many great paintings, obliterated by present-day mechanical methods. A scene of long, long ago, a truly Russian scene, as Tolstoy described in "War and Peace" and "Anna Karenina." The master of the lands drove out to view his harvest, to be among his workers and to call out "Bog pomoshch'" (God's help!). Such moments remembered justify being born just to experience them.

# BACK IN OMSK

After our Czechoslovakian and Serbian allies had freed Omsk from the Bolsheviks, it was safe for our family to return; however, on our arrival we found that there were many changes in the city. Sofia Grigorievna still lived in our home, but little Shurik was died and his mother was not her old self. She was more silent, intent upon her needlework and awaited to hear from her husband who was to come and take her away.

A new stern-faced cook was now in the kitchen, and I was discouraged from visiting her domain by her brisk efficiency. Besides, Mama told me that the new cook was quite literate and had no need of my instruction. I don't think Mama liked her very much, but accepted her services for the time being.

I learned to my great regret that the Rounskys had moved from their home to a much smaller one across town, and when we went to visit them everything seemed very strange. New surroundings somehow did not go with the familiar faces. I particularity minded the loss of their lovely old garden. I also minded being away from Evgoschino and missed Vasilisa Ivanovna. Mama, too, missed the kind and generous old lady and said that Vasilisa Ivanovna had found it very difficult to part with us. We had been a real family to her for a brief while.

I mused on all these changes and partings, too many already in my lifetime and none of them had contributed to any sense of security or permanency. My beloved grandmother was far away, the steamboat had taken us from another friendly shore, and nothing seemed very promising. Winter came on bleakly enough, but all of a sudden tehre was a change, a very definite change in the atmosphere. A feeling of optimism invaded our home bringing with it new energy and reviving our drooping spirits. Papa was appointed to head the Military School in Semipalatinsk. At that time Siberia was holding up well against the Bolsheviks. The Czechs and the Serbs had proven to be competent allies. Semipalatinsk was another city becoming important because of the Trans-Siberian Railroad. We did not know and could not possibly have foreseen that it would be our last place of residence in our Russian-Siberian odyssey.

# SIBERIA—LIFE IN SEMIPALATINSK

Located on the Irtysch River, Semipalatinsk was founded in 1718 as a Russian frontier post, and grew in importance because of the Trans-Siberian Railway. Unlike Omsk, it retained much of its primitive character and was sprinkled with a curious kind of Oriental flavor because of the Tartar and Khirgiz tribes in the North.

If one associates caravans of camels only with the climates of the East, let me shatter the illusion at once. The Khirgiz tribes of the North used camels because they were hardy enough animals to weather the onslaughts of Siberian winters and to draw sleighs across the snowy tundra. Caravans of camels came pulling sleighs loaded with furs and other merchandise and were a familiar sight in the city of Omsk and then Semipalatinsk.

In the outlying areas of Semipalatinsk there were many very wealthy Tartar landowners whose farmlands were vast and rich in produce and who lived like legendary potentates. As the head of Military School and Army Headquarters, Papa was one of the most important men in the city. The military placed him in a position of responsibility and power and he dealt with many people whose interests were in trade, commerce and industry. He had to review and study various petitions, give audiences and approve certain grants. His favors were much sought after and there was the long established custom of tribal bribes, which he abhorred and discourage. Nevertheless, fantastically large melons found their way into our house and were left on the kitchen door stoop. Bolts of silk were sent to Mama by anonymous donors and cages of special breeds of poultry would sometimes be delivered without any message. Papa balked at that, but some of these gifts had to be accepted in order not to reject the good will of their donors.

The house allotted to our family was very large and had a verandah facing a garden. In the back there was a yard with stables, a bathhouse and some other buildings. The real owner lived in a small house beyond the garden. He was an old retired army captain, totally blind, and appeared occasionally wearing an old army coat.

Papa loved horses, and in this area where Tartar breeders produced exceptionally fine steeds, he became the owner of a truly magnificent animal. It came from the stables of one Tartar landowner who was pleased to send out his very best for Papa's use. As a gift it was most definitely not accepted. Papa insisted on buying it. The Tartar landowner, being more cultured than some of his neighbors, finally agreed. I remember that particular landowner.—Tartar, educated in European capitals, speaking many languages, and living with a young sister on a huge estate, which he inherited from his forefathers. The sister was in her late teens, a beautiful dusky girl showing her Tartar heritage by her slanting eyes and high cheekbones. They visited our home, bringing gifts of silks, which the lovely girl charmingly begged Mama to accept, and an invitation to visit their domain.

"You'd better go," Papa said to Mama, "or there will be no end."

We went. Mama and I rode a good distance in our carriage and arrived at a sprawling mansion where the master warmly welcomed us.

I don't remember the visit at all, except for just one thing. In a large room bare of furniture, there was a n enormous sand table. On it the estate and outlying lands were laid out in minute detail. I had never seen anything like it before—the tiny buildings, figures of animals and humans, trees and landmarks fascinated me.

This man, so different from most of his neighbors, had some legitimate grievances concerning his holdings, and Papa was able to resolve some of his problems. His gratitude and appreciation had to be expressed in some way. Papa flatly refused to accept the horse that was offered, so the man appealed to Mama.

"I think you'd better accept it," Mama said to Papa that evening when my ears were over long, "Or, as you have said before, there will be no end. Anyway, what's one horse?"

The little horse, from a most prestigious line of steeds, was delivered to the stables shod with horseshoes of pure silver. It was for the Colonel's little daughter—"to grow up with." The horseshoes were eventually to be removed and changed for regular ones. It was a most exquisite thoroughbred, a mixture of Arab and Tartar breeds. I saw it a couple of times—it was being nurtured in the regiment stables until it came of age. It was outstandingly beautiful—I could not believe that it was mine.

"It is yours. What will you call it?" they asked me.

"Ouragan! (Tempest) I promptly replied. Ouragan—my little fairytale horse, my dream, my love!

Whatever became of it? Did it grow into a beautiful steed, did its memory ever go back to a stable where a wide-eyed child stretched a hand to caress it?

Ouragan—when were you taken out of those sumptuous stables? When were the silver horseshoes removed from your delicate hooves? Who rode you? Who loved you? Who called you by another name?

I can see myself in the never-never days, which did not come to pass.—A young girl bringing sugar or an apple to the stables, feeling the velvety lips over my palm, seeing the beautiful eyes roll toward me, hearing the neigh of pleasure at my approach. And then I can feel the magnificent body under me—trotting, galloping, racing with the wind.

Looking back on it all now, I recognize what a princely gift that was—a high born little horse shod with silver! It was mine for such a brief while, but the memory was for a lifetime.

Mama tried riding a horse from our stable, but gave it up, preferring her outings in a carriage for which we had a pair of grayish horses called "The Blues."

Rigy—the Sorrel—my father's own horse, was a spectacular animal. Although groomed and cared for by others in the military stables, he identified himself with Papa from the very first and they were strongly attached to each other. He was very tall with a beautiful body of burnished red, and had a white star on his forehead. It was rumored that he did not tolerate any other riders except Papa, and whether there was ny truth to the legend was never really proven except in two instances.—When Papa's officer friends begged a loan of Rizhy, they were tossed of his back almost at one. If Papa looked a bit smug at that, I understood perfectly, for I would have felt the same way about Ouragan.

Since Rizhy was stable with the regimental horses along with the pair for our carriage, we telephoned the stables and the horses would be brought around. There was a telephone in the hall of our house, hung over a trunk covered by an Oriental rug. When one made a call, one climbed up on the trunk, cranked the handle and said, "the Military Stables, please." Very often when Rizhy was brought over for Papa and I was in the yard, the groom would put me up on that magnificent steed and walk him up and down the yard until Papa came out. I always tried to have a lump of sugar in my pinafore pocket, and the great horse seemed very gentle in taking it. Towering over me he was a giant, but I had no fear of him, which pleased Papa and the groom. "He knows who's who," the groom would comment.

On one occasion when Papa had to ride across the frozen river to some distant village, he was returning home at dusk. An unexpected thaw had set in during the day and as he was nearing the homeward shore, there was an ominous crack of ice under the hooves. Papa knew that the river was very deep in that area. Very carefully he slackened the reins and held his breath. Rizhy seemed to be aware and became very quiet, freezing in his gait momentarily. I was growing dark rapidly and the ice was cracking. Suddenly it seemed to Papa that Rizhy's muscles were becoming tensed; he seemed to be gathering strength. As delicately as a dance he pivoted slightly, took a great breath, and gave a great leap, scampering onto the bank as the ice gave way. There he stood trembling in every muscle and Papa realized that he was also trembling. He got off, patted and caressed the great horse, kissed his velvet nostrils and talked aloud to it until both of them were calm.

When we departed from Semipalatinsk, Rizhy had to be left behind. Papa hoped that the Tartar landlord claimed him. Both Papa and I were passionately fond of horses—nothing thrilled me as much as to see the drills of the regimental cavalry. Papa was certain that in time I would become a good rider. I am happy that I did not disappoint him in that.—Years and a continent later, when we rode together in Maryland on McDonogh lands, he was pleased with my horseman-ship, and because of the favorable circumstances and friendships there, we were able to ride several times together. It did not happen in Russia. Rizhy and Ouragan never went on companionable rides, but in a way were not denied our dream completely—the Colonel and his daughter did ride together through the woods and trails of McDonogh.

# MY FIRST TEACHER—MARGARITA IVANOVNA

I learned to read very early. Mama taught me the alphabet and how to recognize words and phrases. I loved books and had a great many, some very beautiful ones, which the relatives and friends supplied. I understand that I astonished them with my ability to read lengthy passages and to memorize easily the delightful poems and jingles found in children's books. I suppose it was natural that Mama showed me off a bit, just as later she loved to show off my drawings. Her own love of books, especially poetry, was quite evident. She taught me many poems, some of which I remember to this day.

It was in Semipalatinsk that I acquired my first teacher. Her name was Margarita Ivanovna. She must have been then in her late 50s, and I remember a slim, elegant lady, pleasant-faced, with coifed graying hair and en enamel brooch in the shape of a pansy, which was fastened at the collar of an immaculate blouse. The pansy had a dewdrop of a diamond, and in later years, seeing similar Victorian jewelry, I always recalled Margarita Ivanovna. She was an exceptionally fine teacher, coming, as I later learned, from the highly prestigious Smolny Institute in St. Petersburg. That was a school for aristocratic girls founded by Catherine the Great. I think Margarita Ivanovna had some distant relatives in Semipalatinsk. When the Smolny was taken over by the revolutionary regime in St. Petersburg and its gracious halls of learning were occupied by government offices, she made her way to Seimpalatinsk and was engaged as an instructor there by several families.

She brought much interest and learning into my young life, knowing full well how to deal with youngsters. Sometimes he supplemented her lessons with nature studies, bringing at one time a large shadow box with an exhibit of bees, then an exhibit of ants and butterflies. She was highly pleased with my love for reading and my ability to memorize poems and passages. She taught me grammar in the old classic manner, the way my parents had been taught. At that time there was such innovation in the matter of grammar and several letters of the alphabet were dropped by the Bolsheviks in order to make the orthography "simpler." Later, in the gymnasia in Harbin, China, where I was enrolled, the new grammar was taught and some of the older teachers deplored the "barbaric" innovation. To this day I write a mixture of both pre-Revolutionary and Soviet orthography, which is perhaps the most "barbaric" way of all. However, friends with whom I've corresponded in Russian through the years have assured me that my extensive vocabulary and ability to express myself have overshadowed any errors.

"You write from the heart—like an artist," one friend once told me—"and so it is not a matter of orthography."

My parents showed my teacher every kindness and respect. Our carriage was always went to bring her and to take her home. Mama frequently had her in for tea after the lessons. The lesson hours were never tedious—not that I was particularly bright, but she had a way of making every subject interesting, even mathematics, at which I often carped. She never overwhelmed me with praise of affection, but I was aware of her concern, and her firm dedication and wisdom made a deep impression, challenged me, opened new worlds to me.

I always looked forward to her coming, running out into the hall as soon as I heard the carriage stopping outside, and I would hold her pocketbook as she divested herself of her coat. I heard her say to Mama once—

"It is not always that I am greeted in this way. Some of my pupils hide under the sofas."

And I remember Mama, very young and pretty then, ptting an affectionate arm around Margarita Ivanovna and laughing and saying, "I used to hide under the table myself when the terrible old tutor used to come to instruct me and my sister."

Once Margareta Ivanovna asked me, "What do you wish to be when you grow up?"

"A ballerina, please, Margarita Ivanovna," I answered without hesitation, my mind full of ballets and the fact that I was to take part in a children's performance. I remembered that hs crossed herself and her lips twitched. She said something like, "The Lord takes care of those things."

We had lessons in one of the "spare" rooms of the house. After that Margarita Ivanovna would sometimes take tea with my Mama in the parlor. Sometimes she would linger to hear about the little horse that was obtained for me, and sometimes I would badger her to tell me of the Smolny Institute where she had taught. I was told that my father's war record would allow me entrance into that noble institution.

But we were now in Semipalatinsk. There were dark clouds overhead—unrest, Revolution, each day bringing new unhappy developments. My father's world was crumbling. And still I persisted—

"Margarita Ivanovna, if I study hard band be very good, will I go to the Smolny?"

I know now what she could not look at me. Her velvety eyes sought Mama who had come in to invite her to tea. The diamond dewdrop on the pansy brooch matched the sudden teardrop on her lashes.

If God wills, little one. I God wills."

# THE MEN IN MY EARLY-
# EARLY LIFE

It is not my purpose to clarify or comment upon the complications and upheavals of the political scene of the time. There are volumes and volumes written on the Russian Revolution. I record only that which I remember, that I saw through very young eyes, and that I felt with very immature emotions.

In Omsk Papa had dealing and connections with detachments of some Serbian staff officers, and later I understood that both the Serbs and the Czechs were instrumental in aiding him lead the eschalon train of the regiment's wives and children through Bolshevik-occupied territories to Vladivostok.

And so there were Serbian officers in Omsk and later in Semipalatinsk. Very dashing they were in their colorful uniforms, stumbling gallantly in Russian speech, always very correct and attentive. Being a true "daughter of the regiment" I was always attracted by the military splendor, and so zeroed in on one Stoyan—blazingly blue-eyed, dazzlingly blond, so very, very handsome! He bowed from his waist like a daffodil, kissed my small paw like a courtier, and treated me like a princess. This always with a perfectly straight face with no trace of condescension, which I would have been quick to detect.

At some picnic on an island off the River Irtusch, the invited Servian officers were guests of honor. To show their appreciation, theyemulated love-dazed gallants to the equally appreciative regiment wives, whose husbands looked on with tolerlant amusement. They also sang their national songs at Papa's request, and danced a national dance lined up in a row. That dance, led by Stoyan, won my heart completely, and standing beside Mama I applauded enthusiastically. At the close, Stoyan whirled over to us, dropped on one knee, and presented me his sword with a flourish. I had behind Mama's skirts, but from that day one he was my "cavalier." Whose head wouldn't have been turned.

Another time, when a festival was held in the city gardens, I hed to be dispatched home at the end of the day and Stoyan was delegated to be my escort. We were driven home in our open carriage and Stoyan sat with his arm around me—to keep me from jolting, I suppose. Riding through twon I distinctly remember trying to sit up as tall as possible so as not to be mistaken for a small child. I felt quite elated that this dazzling young officer was escorting me home in style.

Warm friendships existed between the Serbian officers and the regiment officials. I only wish that I knew some of the political machinations that were taking place at the time. Papa did tell an interesting story pertaining to the problems they were confronting:

Before leaving Semipalatinsk, it was necessary to organize a route of travel to Vladivostok. Papa and the Servian officers scourted the countryside to learn which outposts were alredy occupied by the Reds and which secondary roads were still open. On these expeditions Papa posed as one of the Serbians since they had diplomatic and military immunity. He and Stoyan and others came up to one outpost occupied by the Reds in order to obtain a pass. It was the beginning of winter, but the night was unusually warm and lit by an uncertain moon. As they approached the sentry at one of the buildings, Stoyan took off the long woolen scarf that he wore and held it bunched in an outstretched hand. The young sentry snapped to attention, then looked terrified.

"Don't! Don't!" he shouted wildly clutching his rifle and bending to duck.

It was disclosed that in the dim light he had mistaken the folded scarf for a hand grenade and thought that Stoyan was about to throw it. Chagrined, deeply humiliated, and still trembling, he addmitted them to the head of the outpost where they were granted eneded passes.

"I should have given him that scarf to hang himself with," Stoyan commented later.

I often thought about that incident—the warm winter night, the tricky moonlight—the lump of a scarf in Stoyan's hand, and the terror of that young sentry. What times were those!

If Pap's aide-de-camp or adjutant was not as handsome as Stoyan, he was, nevertheless, an important member of our household in Semipalatinsk. His name was Otto Petrovich Strouppe, of German descent and a dedicated and most intelligent young man whose devotion to our family was never forgotten. He lived with us and was very close to Papa. Slender, tall, pleasant-faced and extremely courteous, he fulfilled his duties with tact and discretion far beyond his years according to Papa, and was "worth his weight in gold several times over." Mama was always "Madame" to him, and I was always "Mam'selle." There was nothing he would not do for me to gratify my pleasure. Never losing his youthful dignity he played with me when time permitted, attended to all my whims, and I regarded him as a kind of an indulgent big brother that I could send on errands or comkand to amuse; me. Most of his time was spent with my father at the military headquarters and many times he accompanied him on various trips, but there were instances when Papa was away and Otto Petrovich was left guardian of our house. On some occasions he escorted Mama to various functions, assumed responsibilities, and still had the time and good grace to put up with my prattle and demands.

"Let Otto Petrovich alone," Mama would admonish as I rushed at him with some request on his return from headquarters. "He has been busy all day. Let him rest!"

"Nichevo, (It's nothing) Madame, at your service, Mam'selle. I am not tired." And tired or not he would reel off some magic lantern pictures for me, solve a puzzle that had eluded me all day, and send me off to bed well contented with my small world.

At the dinner table where he took his meals with us, he would thank Mama, then turn to Papa, "Sir," he would say, "I overheard an interesting conversation today," and off they would go to Papa's study.

Papa also had a secretary, a Vassily Vassilich, who was reputed to be a wizard at the typewriter. He came below Pap's waist, a tiny figure of a man no taller than I was at the time. He was also devoted to Papa and did some work for him in our home. Papa thought very highly of him and was privately amused by his diminutive size. For one trip across some frozen rivers Papa had a special fur "envelope" of deerskins made up, into which he placed Vassily vassilich for the cold journey.

Papa would tease me and say that he would marry me off to Vassily Vassilich since he was just my height. I think I balked a little at that, remembering the charm of Stoyan, but I could not help being flattered by the gracious attention paid me by Vassily Vassilich.

It must not be assumed that I was a spoiled brat holding sway over people because of my father's high rank. My parents were gracious and unassuming people, having the ability to get along with most everyone. I was brought to be considerate and mannerly, but I was a solitary only child. When playmates came my way I was inclined to have their good-will rather than to assert myself, and it would not have been in my nature to flaunt any prestige because of attentions paid me by such grownup charmers as Stoyan and Otto Perovich. Moreover, there was another unique factor—in our regiment of many families there was a scarcity of little girls my age. Most of the very young children were boys. If they had sisters, most of them were older or married The little boys I did play with on occasions remain very dim in my memory, although I do recall playing some board games with them. We also watched parades and military drills.

Whatever happened to these young men? When the eschalon of wives and children was organized under my father's leadership for the escape farther into Siberia, Stoyan and other officers parted company with Papa. Otto Petrovich was also left behind and joined the regiment of the Black Hussars, which tried valiantly to stem the tide of Revolution. Vassily Vassilich also remained in Semipalatinsk. We heard no more of them once we reached the boundaries of Mongolia. We often wondered—did they survive, perish, or flee the country? Particularly we thought of Otto Petrovich.

"I am at your service, Madame!"

"Sir, I overheard an interesting conversation today!"

Stoyan and Vassily Vassilich lived in our hearts. And if this is any kind of tribute to those dedicated young men who served their country and our family, I am happy to make their names known.

# A BALLERINA FOR A DAY

In Semipalatinsk, Mama had many social obligations, was a gracious and competent hostess, and was warmly received by the circle of officers' wives, but she had
very few close friends. I think she missed my grandmother and family friends
back in Zhitomir. Everything in Siberia was different—its cities grew with its
railroads, the raw and primitive atmosphere of the former frontier posts still prevailed, the climate was harsher, and the cultural elements, according to the delicately bred ladies who found themselves there, were very limited. However, most
of them made the best of it, maintained gracious homes and dispensed hospitality
with good will.

There was a most pleasant lady with a little boy called Yuri who was brought
over sometimes to play with me, but he was several years younger and I don't
recall that we had much in common. There was another officer's wife with a girl
named Milochka, about my age. She was a sulky, spoiled brat, ill mannered and
snobbish. I remember Mama admonishing me with "Don't you be like
Milochka." Yuri was very docile and no fun, but Milochka was always difficult, so
my playmates were disappointing, but I was used to being on my own.

Sometimes I was taken to a public "children's garden" where games were organized and where young women in charge supervised various activities. I don't
think I enjoyed those activities very much.

At the end of the summer there was an event eliciting much excitement—a
costume party for the children. All were to come in costumes, play games, have
refreshments, and prizes were to be rewarded for the best costumes.

"What would you like to be? Mama asked me.

"A ballerina!"

Mama and Yuri's mother put their heads together. Yuri was already marked to
go as a "chertyonok"—a little devilish imp, all red and black with small horns on
his head and a forked tail dangling from his rear. His mother, being very creative,
took charge of my costumes also. From yards of pink satin a "tutu" was fashioned
and frothed over with veiling from Mama's wedding veil. There were white silk
tights, pink ballet slippers, and a huge bow of moiré ribbon tied at the waist. My

78

hair was combed in the style of a Degas ballerina, and I was naturally, ecstatic! I could not think of anything else for days.

The great day came, and Yuri was brought over, very engaging in his scarlet costume. I was dressed, breathless with excitement, and we drove out to the gardens. Among other children we found Milochka who was wearing a gorgeous costume of a blue butterfly with gauzy spangled wings. I thought she was beautiful and told her so, but she only frowned at me.

As I recall there were many games, refreshments, then everyone formed in a line for the Grand March while a band played a judges deliberated. I don't remember any of the other costumes. I do know that Yuri, Milochka and I marched around and around before the judges. The prizes were then announced and at each announcement the band played a flourish and the judge came down the steps of the platform to award the prize. Yuri got the first prize—a large silk bag filled with candy. Milochka was the second prize—a similar bag of candy. I was awarded the third prize—a silk bag containing an enormous apple! I was in heaven.

We were surrounded by children and people who congratulated us. Then the games continued. They formed a ring and danced while the band played. I was suddenly pushed into the center of the ring, and several voices cried out to me, "Dance! Dance for us! You are the ballerina!"

I don't know where my courage came from. I was alone within a huge ring of clapping spectators and the band was playing. Yet away I went. The music and the clapping made me do what I had never done before. I never had a dance lesson in my life, but I turned into the ballerina of my dreams for a few magical moments.

Mama said later that she couldn't believe her eyes. She had been talking to some people outside the ring when loud cheers and clapping broke out. Looking up she saw her daughter pirouetting and whirling like a small pink dervish. It was something she had never seen before. She enjoyed telling that story throughout the years. Always amazed at my daring for I was not a forward child.

Despite my love for the dance, ballet lessons were few and far between. In later years I did dance with an ensemble in amateur theatricals, and I did delight my father on several occasions by performing for him my own version of the can-can.

"Why do you love the ballet so? he once asked me.

"Because my soul seems to dance when Is ee them perform."

I was no longer a child when I made that statement, but if I were asked today, I would give the same reply. I think my intense interest was noted very early and to give my parents full credit, I must say that if they could not arrange ballet lessons, they did provide the possibility for me to attend many notable performances.

# MORE ABOUT
# SEMIPALATINSK, SIBERIA

I was too young to understand fully the political upheavals taking place in Russia at the time. The grownups talked mostly about things beyond my comprehension and used names that would later be written into history books. Often I sensed tension or an unusual soberness in my parents. While an apprehensive kind of atmosphere sometimes permeated the household, for the most part my days in Semipalatinsk were pleasant and orderly. There were lessons with Margarita Ivanonva, rides in the carriage with Mama, and visits to the summer residences—the dachas—of other staff members. There were garden festivals, picnics and always so much to observe! The true meaning of the word "Bolsheviks" was still not clear to me. Much, much earlier I seem to have had a fear of "the Germans,—that must have been during the days of World War I in another part of Russia. There had been a huge world map hanging on a wall in some room with an array of colored pins stuck in various places. Dimly I recall being cautioned never to touch or move those pins "or the Germans would come."

I found the world around me quite fascinating. Beyond the garden the landlord had some chicken coops and even a pigpen. When there was a litter of piglets, I was enchanted and wanted one for a pet, even though I was quite satisfied with the long haired cat called "Kichka" who came with the house and readily adopted me. "Kichka" was a fine playmate, but as the piglets grew pinker and chubbier, I could not keep awaay from the pigpen. Greatly daring, one day I leaned over and scooped up the nearest little animal who wiggled and squealed at the top of his lungs while; his mother grunted disapproval. I ran with him through the gardens to our verandah where Mama was serving tea to a couple of ladies. The piglet broke away and ran into the house where he was chased and caught by the cook. I expected to be punished, but the ladies including Mama, broke into gales of laughter. Mama often lamented the fact that she could not have a picture of me with the squealing little pig in my arms running straight into her elegant tea party.

Beyond our back yard, separated by a wooden fence, there was another large residence more rustic than ours. A vegetable garden was laid out in near patterns just below, and by climbing up a few beams I could look down and see everything. Toward late afternoon the owner and his family would come out and tend it, watering the young plants, weeding and hoeing. Their activities were of great interest to me, and as the summer progressed I was able to follow the ripening of their produce. In late summer, hanging over the fence, I could see a perfect picture of a bountiful harvest brought about by their daily work and care. Squashes and melons were removed from the vines, potatoes dug, beans gathered, carrots pulled. I felt a kind of pride for those people, and sensed also that the earth itself was giving me a lesson—work the soil, treat it well, and the reward is in a rich harvest.

With equal unflagging interest I observed the people around me. A few faces surface again and again in my memory over the years. Although a few officers in the Military School and Headquarters outranked Papa, who then had the rank of Colonel, it is my understanding that he worked with them in complete harmony and was well liked and respected. Mama was young and inexperienced, but had a way of charming people and her position as "the Staff Commandant's wife presented no problems. The leading hostess, a general's lady and reputed to be something of a dragon, was completely disarmed by Mama and bent over backwards to welcome her, shower hospitality upon her and advise her discretely.

The general's family name was Sokolnitsky. There were two grown daughters, Olga and Nina, and a teenager son Oleg. Olga was a dusky, petulant beauty already engaged to an officer; Nina, chubby and jolly was still having lessons. Oleg was a prankster who shocked the family with his peccadilloes, although the general, his father, regarded his antics with a wary eye.

The general's lady, having practically adopted Mama, was always doing something for her pleasure and mine. Once she mentioned a folio of paper dolls, which she thought would amuse me. Even now I can recall that kindly, slightly overblown lady putting her hand to her brow and muttering earnestly, "God give me memory. Where ever did I stash away those things?"

Apparently God helped. The folio was found and handed over to me. Oh, the bliss! There were ladies and gentlemen with wardrobes and wardrobes of exquisite costumes. What hours of joy followed in dressing them and organizing events and festivities in which they took part. As a rule I did not play with dolls much, but paper dolls were something else. An element of creativity was there and that was what appealed to me.

The Sokolnitskys occupied a large elaborate house, which we often visited. Sometimes the younger daughter Nina would play with me, but the older beauty Olga appeared seldom, coming and going in beautiful outfits, leaving a trail of lovely perfume in her wake and condescendingly patting my cheek as she sped by. The chubby sister Nina was a volunteer in the local military hospital where she was in great demand because of her sunny disposition and winning ways with the convalescents. Not to be outdone, the beautiful Olga offered her services there also, but could not take the "horrors" of attending some post-operative patients. It was reported that she fainted dead away at the sight of blood, and fled home as soon as she recovered.

"Oh, well," I heard Papa remark when mama told him of the incident, "some talents are for the battlefield, some others for the bedroom!" Naturally, I did not understand, but the beauteous Olga did not appear to me as wonderful as before.

It seemed to me that my parents were always in complete agreement with each other, and I was aware of the affection between them.—The way Papa deferred to Mama, and the way she sought to implement his position. I was never awware of any differences between them except in small matters, as, or instance the choice of a corsage for a festival.

"Take the larger one," Papa pressed holding out florist's boxes. "It will be more noticeable on your gown."

"But I prefer the smaller one. It is more gragrant and I will enjoy it more."

Once he put a fabulous six-strand pearl necklace around her throat. He had bought if from the Tartars who had fortunes in pearls. They stood in front of a tall mirror admiring it, and noticing me in the background, Mama turned to me clasping the necklace.

"For you—one day you will have it."

That necklace later paid part of our passage to America. Never being fond of pearls I did not regret it. Actually I have never had much love for precious gems. The exceptions would be those few, which my husband set for me into my engagement ring and my wedding cross. Diamonds, my birthstones, I did not alike at all and never owned any except a chip in a stock-pin.

As I said before, Oleg, the general's son was a prankster, but he was not all bad. Very often when we visited he entertained me with his antics and I was a most appreciative audience. His feats of gymnastics seemed spectacular—standing on his head, turning endless summersaults and leap-froging over his mother's elegant furniture. He was a generous boy, too, and frequently would pull out a box of caramels from his pocket and offer them to me, saying, "Why take one? Take two!"

His sisters regarded him as a horror, but I don't recall anything that was really objectionable. I like him, and we got along extremely well. He joined the troupe of young scouts, which was formed after the organization of American Scout Troupes by a young man who had traveled in America. The scouts in Semipalitinsk were allotted a small island near town, where a summer camp was set up. I think Papa was responsible for its welfare, and as it was something entirely new, much interest was shown in the organization.

I remember being taken to see the camp, and admired the young people in their uniforms, their manner of saluting their officers and the curious tents in which they lived. Naturally I also longed to become a scout. "Later! Later!" Mama consoled me.

It was generally agreed tha tin joining the Scouts Oleg became greatly "improved." However, since I had never found any fault where he was concerned, I wondered what "improvement" really meant.

Many events, many faces come to mind as I try to look deep into the Semipalatinsk period. A contingent of American officers were guests of the Military Headquarters, and were entertained by Papa and his staff. I do not know how or why they came there. Among them was a Captain Grady, who spoke a little Russian and he and Papa became fast friends. When parting came both men were somewhat emotional for they had enjoyed a friendship which overcame barriers of language, They had admired each other's qualities and fjound much common ground. Embracing his friend at the train, Papa unfastened the collar of his tunic, and removing his baptismal gold cross, gave it to Grady. Much moved, Grady opened the collar of his tunic and tried to remove the silver image of Lucifer, the seal of his Masonic order, which he wore on a chain. He wanted Papa to have it.

""I can't take it! Give me this," and Papa pointed to the USA metal insignia on the collar of Grady's uniform.

"I understand. Of course you can't I'm an idiot!" Grady then tore the insignia off his collar and closed my father's hand on it.

That USA insignia remains today encased with my father's regimental decorations. Captain grady resided in San francisco, and when we came to America and landed there, he was the first to greet us at the dock and to welcome us to America. He tried to persuade my father to make his home in San Francisco There were many opportunities to study the language and work for we were among the first White Russians to arrive. However, my fahter's brother, Constantin Seletzky, the former Russian Embassy priest, resided with his family in Baltimore and awaited our arrival. I have often wondered what ourlife would have been like had we stayed in San Francisco among those welcoming and caring people. Our destinies were forges on anvils of harsh reality, but perhaps that was what gave us stamina to survive.

A particular moment during our last days in Semipalitinsk is retained in my memory. An officer from the headquarters staff was being transferred to another post. A farewell picnic with all officers in attendance was held in a birch grove outside the city. It was toward the end of summer on a beautiful golden afternoon. Several brass samovars were set to boiling in the clearing, rugs were spread, and picnic fare brought out from the carts that had come earlier. Orderlies and valets bustled about, bumped into each other nd clowned obligingly for the benefit of children who stood around while their elders surrounded the departing quest of honor. There was a slight refreshing breeze, which rustled through the birches. Suddenly I overheard a voice speaking in a tone not consistent with the joyous occasion.

"Sirs! Sirs!" a young officer was saying to one group of his comrades. "Do you realize that the execution is taking place right now. It is unbelievable that it is happening. How can it be possible? How can it be borne?"

"How can it be possible?" echoed the trees overhead.

I saw Papa and the guest of honor walk away together and stand a little distance apart surveying the gay picnic scene. They stood in silence, looking very severe, as if they wanted to imprint something in their minds. I have never seen a public execution, but I imagine that before the doomed man is blindfolded, he looks for the last time with a similar gaze on all that he is about to leave.

# GO WITH GOD

In the last autumn of our stay in Semipalatinsk events culminating in our departure occurred ceaselessly; soon accelerating their pace and eventually turning into a maelstrom, which absorbed us all.

Ever since the assassination of the Imperial family, a kind of blight had seemed to fall on everything. Shocked to the core, outraged, guilt-ridden with a false sense of guilt simply because they themselves still survived. The counter-revolutionaries, the men loyal to Imperial Russia, the Whites, found themselves in a traumatic situation within a chaotic state of government.

Papa was like that—cut to the heart and hurting. He still fulfilled his obligations, knew himself to have definite responsibilities, and acted according. I have often thought of his personal anguish at the time. He was a young man and the burdens placed upon him just have been staggering. Yet he continued with his secret missions, organized detachments, planned impossible coups—anything and everything to stem the tide of Bolshevism.

I do not know just when it was decided that we would have to leave Semipalatinsk. By "we," I mean Mama and me, and the wives and children of the military along with older family members. The men were needed to remain for resistance. The Bolsheviks, who held power over Moscow and a large part of European Russia, faced this resistance from parties whose supporters ranged from Socialist Revolutionaries to tsarists, and the resulting civil was ws further complicated by foreign intervention. The main areas of warfare between the Whites and the Reds were: South Russia and the Caucases; the Ukraine, involving Germany, France and Poland; the North, involving the British, French and the United States; the Baltic States, where the White Army and the free corps battled the Reds; and Siberia, where General Kollchak set up a government and tried to hold things in control. Bad communication and cooperation among the White leaders gave the Reds the advantage. IT was also in the present interests of the Czechs to ally themselves to our cause, and to give us passage under their protection until a safer place was reached.

Late in the fall when there were frosts and snows, definite preparations for our departure were made. Papa, of course, was organizing the echelon, which, it was hoped, would carry us out to Vladivostok. It was to be composed of many freight cars outfitted with bunks and heating so that women and children could travel during the long winter journey. A Czech crew was to man the train so that it would be possible to pass through Red-occupied territories. Besides, Papa's foresight and former connections provided the exhelon with first rate engineers and mechanics. There were other families to be evacuated beside the military—those of city officials and residents. Some were to disembark at various points to join relatives and friends or to make other connections.

Lessons with Margarita Ivanovna were discontinued, although she came frequently to the house and became a great source of comfort to Mama. Packing caused great disruption in the house and crates and trunks were everywhere.

"Where's Vladivostock?" I asked. It was pointed out on a map—a large meaningless dot near China.

"Talk to her," Papa appealed to Mama catching me in a hug, which bruised my cheek against the buttons of his uniform.

Mama talked—oh, how she talked!—She spoke of Vladivostok, so distant, but safe and different; spoke of the train on which we would ride with many friends—such a different kind of train; spoke of the places we would pass, villages and little towns—such a different journey it was to be!

I think it was the use of her word "different" that made me wary, and her somewhat erratic speech, as though her mind was elsewhere. We could only take one trunk with us, but my bear Mishka was already packed in it, as well as a coupled of dolls. I didn't care about the dolls, but had to be reassured that Mishka had been included. Mama went on to talk about the people who would be with us—little Yuri and his mother as well as other children.

"And Papa?"

"Papa joins us later—maybe in Vladivostok, maybe sooner. Pray hard that he will be safe. Pray hard every night!"

No one had any answers to my frequent questions and sometimes people pretended not to hear.

"What about Ouragan? What about Papa's Rizhy?"—whatabout—whatabout—

There was so much activity and confusion in the house, people came and went. The tailor arrived with coats for the journey. They were "shubas" the fur-lined winter coats that everyone wore. Mama's was of maroon wool lined with fox fur. Mine was dark blue lined with a fur of a samml, squirrel-like Siberian animal, reddish in color, called "koulonok." I liked it although it came down to my ankles. A few days after it was delivered Mama had me trying it on again. I did not mind as it felt good and warm. As I took it off, I felt a kind of stiffness in the upper part of its back under the fur lining. Something like paper had been sewn into it. I learned alter that a few precious documents like the Tsar's Gramota and the Record of Service in the Imperial Army had been stitched into the back portion of my coat. I learned, too, that Mama had a special belt with pockets to wear under her garments, containing some gold coins and a few pieces of jewelry.

Today, carefully preserving the stained old papers, rereading the wonderful formal phrases imprinted on them, it still seems unbelievable that once I carried them on my back and lived with them daily through a long and hazardous winter. Did I have any thoughts or feelings concerning them?—I think I began to accept everything as it came, and only years later, reflecting on all events, I had an intense commiseration for the child bearing on its back a burden of old documents.

"When you were playing with dolls, I was riding in a cattle-car," I used to think privately and a bit savagely later in life when faced with my peers in America. They would be girls from well-established homes who found my background "unusual" or "exciting" and pressed me for details, but I was reluctant to reveal most of it.

Peering at night into the Siberian skies thickly studded with stars, I picked out the Great Dipper—the only constellation I knew—and continued to observe and listen. I was not in anyone's way and I roamed the house freely, observing the changes taking place. Sometimes I was sent out to the bare garden, but always crept back to the kitchen doors from which vantage point I could see people coming and going in the courtyard. I saw Papa once come riding in, flinging himself off his great horse and calling one of the orderlies to attend to it. I had no sugar in my coat pocket, but I picked my way across the snowy yard and went up to Rizhy. The man holding him was not the groom who gave me rides before, and seeing me approach, called out a warning, "Don't get too near, barishnya! He's a lively one!"

Yet, as I came toward them Rizhy reached toward me, and to the groom's amazement bent his head while I stroked his nostrils. He sniffed my mittened palm, blew on it, and I hope, forgave me for finding it empty. That was the last time I saw Rizhy.

As I mentioned before, the telephone in our hall hung over a trunk covered with a Caucasian rug. Mama, being small, always knelt on it to talk. I recall coming upon her as she was answering a call, and the next moment I was horrified to see her tumbling off in a faint. I think I screamed and Margarita Ivanovna, who was in the house, rushed in. Mama recovered in a few minutes, cried a little, and was apologetic for giving us a fright. She had just had the news that Papa had been unanimously elected by his staff to be the leader of the echelon that was to take us away. That was the first time I saw Mama give way. She who had dealt so competently with numerous problems had found the great good news too much!

Margarita Ivanovna, ministering to Mama, crossed herself again and again. "Thanks be to God," she kept repeating. "You will not be separated; he will be with you. O course they elected him! Who else is as capable?"

Both of them huddled on the floor by the trunk, and I was hugged and petted by both.

"Go thank God, little one," Margarita Ivanovna sniffed at me, and so I went off to kneel before Archbishop Anthony's icon.

These pages are written primarily for people I love and of whose affection I am aware. Therefore I am not ashamed to record the tears, the fears. They will understand and not think me maudlin.

I don't know how other regimental wives felt about leaving their husbands, but the confidence they had in Papa's leadership and judgement, gave some measure of security and hope to them. I do know that Mama spent a great deal of time helping and advising other families. There were many speculations concerning the weather. Would it be a severe Siberian winter with snows and gales? Would the freezing cold across the white endless plains add tot he problems fo the evacuees? Would the storms sweeping from the north hamper the progress of the train? The weather seemed to be of mor concern than the advancement of the Red armies.

Days rushed by—then came one early evening.—Snow on the ground—not very cold—sleighs with horses sout in the courtyard. Many people bustling around, servants, neighbors. Muffled in my new coat, with new felt boots on my feet, I stood by Mama while people hugged us, kissed us, made the sign of the cross over us. A furry shape streaked out fo the house, rubbing against my legs. It was Kichka, the large Siberian cat who played with me so often. I picked her up and kissed her cold nose. The kind woman who sometimes looked after me ran out with a necklace of oven-warm boobliki. She hung them around my neck and pressed her tear wet cheek to mine. The fragrance of bake dough permeated the atmosphere. Someone picked me up, tucked me under a rug beside Mama in the sleigh. The coachman removed his fur hat and crossed himself before picking up the reins.

"S Bogom! (Go with God)" someone cried, and we rode out of our gates into the darkening night.

# THE JOURNEY

Unfamiliar and sinister situations are difficult to describe. One can either become too dramatic or perhaps too bland in presenting verbally the scenarios that were played out on our winter journey.

I had seen trains before in bustling well-lit stations with crowds that were fun to observe—people meeting and greeting each other, obsequious porters moving mounds of baggage, sometimes a gay burst of music welcoming someone. Trains had been like jolly oversized toys—neat, important little engines emitting comical toots and panting in happy exuberance, drawing after them a string of pretty gleaming cars. What I saw when we reached the station were huge monsters, threatening and ungainly, belching dirty yellow steam into the frosty air, grinding metal upon metal with ear-splitting sounds, sending shafts of blinding light through the gloom as though searching out their prey. The enormous wheels terrified me as we passed them. And the station itself was like some underground cavern, dimly lit, soiled by snow brought in from the streets and gusted by icy drafts from one end to the other, and filled to overflowing with a dark mass of humanity—shadows pressing on shadows, their apprehensions permeating the claustrophobic atmosphere.

The monstrous engine past which we were escorted had no attachment of passenger cars equipped with comforts to accommodate travelers. It drew a long line of boxcars used to transport cattle or freight—cars with huge sliding central doors and perhaps an aperture set high on the opposite sides. Somewhere near the engine were freight cars with coal, provisions and baggage.

The boxcar assigned to us was somewhere in the middle of a train that contained about thirty cars. Our boxcar was to accommodate eight women with small children and one very old retired general. Papa had done his best for the evacuees, and these cars were luxurious compared to the bareness of some later ones that we encountered. Berths were nailed up and deerskins lined the walls. In the center was a small cast iron stove with a chimney pipe going up through the roof. Mama occupied one of the central lower berths and I had the smaller narrow one just above her. It had a guardrail of rough wood. Yuri and his mother shared a large lower berth together. Above them was the elderly daughter of the general. He had a berth across the car opposite ours. Other spaces were occupied by women with children. The women lined their berths with pillows and blankets, putting up wool shawls or plaids at night for privacy. There were lamps with candles for light, and daylight came through a small window above the general's berth. There was no space or place for Papa, and it was understood that he was to bunk with the engineers.

We settled into our quarters as best we could. Hand luggage was alongside of everybody's berth; it was very crowded. There were no sanitary accommodations—one had to depend on the surreptitious uses of small chamber pots. To wash, one melted snow in basins on the stove where one also boiled teakettles. One waited hopefully for a stop in some village or town where one could go to a bathhouse, if time permitted. The jolting and jerks of the train caused the crude cars to creak and groan. The ceaseless harsh rattle of the wheels drowned out conversation. It was not too cold with the stove going, but I do remember waking time and again with my hair frozen to the pillow and of bundling up beside Yuri in his berth to play board games or to draw. His mother was a lady with inexhaustible imagination. She spun stories by the hour to diver the children, drew pictures on scraps of paper, and invented games. She was small, thin, rather plain in looks, but when she gathered the children around her and told her stories above the noisome wheel-rattle, everyone tried to get as close as possible to Auntie." Her name totally escapes me, except the surname, which was Lekomtsev.

Mama tells that in the close confines the ladies deferred to the old general who, it must be said to his credit, bore stoically his discomforts and lack of privacy. We saw Papa rarely. When the train stopped at some station he would dash in, greet everyone, tell us how long we were stopping, and dash out again. He never ate with us or lingered. His former uniform was gone and he wore the drab one of the Czechs.

Yuri and I became more friendly. He was not well that winter and his mother did not take him out for walks when the train was standing. He stayed in his bunk under the blankets, and together we drew endless pictures with colored pencils of which we had a good supply. I was the better artist, but he had more imagination, and together we collaborated on all manner of scenes. Sometimes, imitating the grownups, we played cards or tried to build card houses—an impossible feat because of the jolting. There seemed to be no problems with the children—no whimpering or tantrums, no admonishments from the elders. On the contrary, we were often told that we behaved like "big people," that our fathers would be prouds of us, and the like. I think we were subdued but certainly not cowed by the environment in the early days of our journey. The old general was tolerant, but his spinster daughter in her bunk above Yuri, was irritable and morose. She had been a gymnasia teacher of the upper grades, and was not used to small children. Once when I was constructing a paper house for Yuri, she climbed down from her berth, sweeping my structure with her skirt. I protested in frustration. She thought me very rude and complained to Mama, who made me apologize at once. However, when Christmas came, which we spent transit, she was very adept in teaching us how to cut paper stars, snowflakes and decorative chains out of old newspapers for the small fir tree that my father delivered to our car. Moreover, she snipped some bead tassels from some garment in her valise and hung them on the tree. Fortunately they jingled in time to the rattling wheels.

The echelon stopped at villages and sometimes we went out to their market places, usually held under low sheds of rough timber. Provisions were scarce. We had enough to eat, however, the main meals, simple as they were, were supplied in tin containers from the kitchen car. Milk and dairy products were in short supply and had to be obtained from the villages. When the train stopped we wrapped up and went to walk alongside the cars. Often the villages were no more than a huddle of huts banked by a forest. Sometimes the inhabitants would come out toward us to sell some milk or baked goods, which always intrigued us. In the frosty air the fragrance of freshly baked bread or pirozhki was tantalizing. Sometimes there were pies of cabbage and meat or large rectangular bake sheets. The peasant women, dressed in their shawls and sheepskins coats offered their wares, lifting the clean linen towels with which the goods were covered. There were also the inevitable "boobliki," hung around the necks of some women. Shaggy country dogs would frolic around wagging their plumed tails, and the children, starved for the companionship of pets, would quickly befriend them despite maternal warnings.

I don't remember any of the echelon children except little Yuri, and on one rare occasion when he was permitted to go outside, he made friends with a great ungainly village dog. Standing stiffly in his thick fur-lined coat, his small pinched face hardly visible within the fur cap, he awkwardly patted the huge beast and fed him most of the pirozhok which his mother had bought him. When the time came to part, Yuri suddenly burst into tears, and as he was led back to the car, the dog retreated, emitting mournful little howls. I don't know why, but I started to cry, too. That evening little Yuri was too despondent to play games with me.

On our outings we met some children from other freight cars occasionally. There was one little girl who collected wax drippings from candles. She carried them in a small box and later showed us what she did with them. I was enchanted to see tiny roosters, cats, rabbits and foxes modeled by her from candle wax. She took a liking to Yuri and presented him with a wax mouse that had a long string tail.

Not to be outdone, I tried my hand at wax modeling, too, but had no success Moreover, I was advised to stick to my drawing, and when the old general commissioned me to make him a drawing of a ballerina, I was in my glory. I drew him a dancer to end all ballerinas and he was very pleased. He even pinned it over his berth and showed it to others. I couldn't quite understand the amusement of the grown ups when he sighed and rolled his eyes, saying, "Ah! Such beautiful little legs! It warms the blood to look!"

Emboldened by my success, I asked Mama if I should draw him a "rousalka"—a water maiden, but Mama choked a little and said "God forbid!" So Yuri and I continued the pictorial adventures of a certain Imperial House, inspired by his wax model.

There are many blurs in my memory concering the first lap of our journey, but I do rmember that snow covered everything. It was deep winter—a "refugee's winter" someone called it. However, there were no gales or bitter frosts. Some little villages where we stopped were very peaceful, in others there had been uprisings put down by the dispatched Reds. In several places trains full of Red soldiers stood in the stations, and we learned that our mechanics were pressed into service to repair the locomotives of the Bolsheviks. This way we gained passage, but the progress became slower. Stops were longer as we went on.

Sometimes we stood for days in the stations among other trains the voices of the elders were low discussing events. Mama looked very concerned most of the time. She saw very little of my father. In recalling things later, she confessed, "I never knew where he was, and every time the train started up again I could only hope and pray that he was on it." He slept and ate just anywhere at any time and he was forced to acquiesce to the necessity of long stops while the mechanics were commandeered to service the Bolsheviks.

Sensitive and observant, I began to feel the tense atmosphere, to recognize that the groups of soldiers milling around the trains were Red Army men, and to be aware that the women in the freight cars took pains to make themselves unobtrusive whenever they stepped out. Even in Siberia, where the climate made certain demands upon prevailing fashions, the ladies of the regiment wore hats—fur-trimmed, it is true, but still fashionable. Now the women wrapped their heads in plain shawls, pulling them close around their faces. All of them also wore felt boots called "valenki," instead of the former elegant footgear. They melted into the crowds of peasant women and other nondescript travelers. I don't recall that any were ever molested. They always kept their children close by their side and never raised their voices.

Once Mama, having ventured out at one station for some milk, returned with an ashen face. Her hands trembled as she handed the jug to someone and took off her shawl.

"Two of them—young men with rifles stopped me—called me a rude name and asked where I got the milk. I just pointed toward the market and dived past them—they even laughed and jeered." She was very agitated.

Later we hd the news that the large village we were approaching had an uprising and a detachment of Reds had been sent to suppress it. It was hoped that we would not have to stop there long. When the train did halt, our doors were flung open by some soldiers. They were civil enough, even waved to the children huddled around "Auntie," but ordered our doors to stay open. Donning our coats, we obeyed and peered outside at the station.

The generals daughter standing by the doors, kept up a running commentary in a low voice on events taking place—

"The place is crawling with them—all armed to the teeth—they took the station master away just now—I heard they have the village head. Look, now, look,—that must be the one—they've hurt him, and they're taking him away!"

I was near her where I could see. A group of soldiers were prodding an elderly man with their rifles. His head was roughly bandaged and his long white hair was red with dripping blood.

A sudden panic seized me, a feeling of such utter hopeless despair, that I became hysterical for the first time in my life. Someone snatched me and someone slid the doors shut despite the orders. Another person said that there were rifle shots, but Iw as too sick to hear anyting and my hysteria set off Yuri and the other children. I suppose the accumulations of strain became too much for us, snatched as we were from familiar surroundings not so long ago. It was not just fear that I felt—it was the realization that all known peace and order were no more, that each day was grayer than the one before, and that on one could give any credible reassurance as to any future improvement.

# THE ARSENAL OF FEAR

In Mama's quite illustrious family there was an uncle, General Vladimir Osk-arovich Kappel, who, after distinguishing himself in World War I, became active as one of the main White leaders under Admiral Kolchak during the Revoution. Due to his activities there was little communication between him and Mama, but after the exodus of the refugees from Semipalatinsk, their paths crossed briefly, but during a ghastly catastrophe. Both shared the horrors of the historic explosion at Achinsk when the Bolsheviks blew up a train and killed hundreds of people.

There is a book about my uncle, which was written in Russian by A. Fedorov-ich and printed in Melbourne, Australia. It is entitled "General V. O. Kappel." His leadership of a White army is fuly documented and his genial and heroic personality fairly shines from the pages. He is noted for routing the Reds from several cities along the Volga River in 1918, outwitting them in various ways to achieve his victories. Later he served as commander of another White Army in Urals under the leadership of Admiral Kolchak. His daring and talent achieved many triumphs and the heartfelt devotion of his men. When his horse fell through a frozen river and his legs were injured, his allegiance to duty made him refuse to abandon the cause. Eventually he perished from blood poisoning. That a book should have been written by one of his officers shows the devotion of his soldiers.

At Achinsk, Siberia, half way to Manchuria, it so happened that the train, which General Kappel was commandeering, would be stationed alongside of ours. Papa knew of the general's proximity, and, while he was unable to make immediate contact, he thought up a plan that would bring them together later.

Arriving at the large Achinsk station in the early morning, Papa, as he told it, was dismayed by the congestion of trains that had arrived and kept on arriving with evacuees, battalions of soldiers and freight. Such crowds always had a claustrophobic effect on him, another trait that I inherited. When he learned that there would be a long delay at Achinsk, he arranged for our train to pull out on a siding outside the center of the city.

We left the station in mid-morning and came to rest on a slight incline from which the city was dimly visible. It was a mild, overcast gray winter day and snow was everywhere. To my delight, we had an outing, the pleasure of which was heightened by Papa's presence. He walked the line of cars, talked to people, and returned again and again to be with us. The railroad tracks to the right and left of us made a veritable network on the snowy plain. I have never to this day seen so many rails. When one is small, everything seems bigger, but having traveled a bit during my life, I have never seen a rail center as large as that at Achinsk. With Papa near us, mama's spirits were high, and walking between them, sinking and being pulled out of the snowdrifts, I sensed again the feeling of security.

Back in our car, it was around noon that distant booming sounds brought everyone to the doors. Looking back toward the city they saw what looked like a fiery cloud. Almost at once, it seemed, trains from the distant terminal began to pull out toward us. "They came," Papa related later, "as though activated by the sudden blast—and in their wake hordes of people on foot were fleeing in mindless panic!"

In a very short space of time the tracks around us were completely filled with echelons, while a great fire seemed to be raging in the distance. Of the turmoil around I was not a witness, but the constant reports brought in gave a terrifying picture of what went on outside. Partly destroyed cars, mutilated people, distracted officials and other survivors formed a crazed mass in the middle of snowy plains. The din of locomotives, roar of voices, shrieks and groans penetrated the walls of our wagon. They said many people had perished, hundreds were injured, having been thrown out of cars with debris. They said that our train, along with General Kappel's had been standing very near the explosive freight.

"Saved by God," Papa said later when someone commented on the fortunate decision to pull out of the crowded station. "Spared and saved by God!"

Shaken as they were, it was impossible for the travelers of our echelon not to venture out, and they came back with more tales of horror. Teams of sleds as well as Red Cross trains brought out the survivors and the wounded. Tents were hastily set up in the clearings, bonfires burned through the night. Speculations ran rife. It was said that the station beyond us was in shambles, littered with dismembered bodies. An anguished night brought an equally anguished murky dawn.

From the book on General Kappel I have made the following translation of the event as documented by a Colonel Viropaev, attached to the general's staff and traveling with him.

"The army train of General Kappel"s staff slowly moving eastward, arrived at the city of Achinsk. The echelon stood east of the center. A little past its center stood three cisterns with benzene. A few tracks to the north from the cisterns, in the very center of the standing echelons, stood two wagons loaded with black gunpowder, formerly designated for the hunters in the Kamchatka region. The cisterns stood approximately twenty wagons away from us. I was composing a telegram at a small table near the window. The commandant, General Kappel, was giving audience to some heads of trains, a usual staff-day procedure. But at twelve noon or a bit later, I heard a short hum and then two thundering blasts, at which the thick glass windows of our salon-car crashed inward together with their frames. I was literally pressed face down into the table by the gusts of air, and the first thing I heard amidst the flying debris, was the calm voice of Kappel—'Are you alive? Give me my gun.' I took up the gun and straddling the shards of glass on the floor handed it to Kappel who was already leaving. Descending the steep steps of our car, we saw heave doors and fragments of cars hurtling down from above. The doors of freight cars, falling at an angle upon frozen ground were imbedded in it for more than a yard—such was the force. The ehat from the roaring flames leaping upward made us turn to the rear of our echelon and witness several lines of burning cars filled with writhing, still living people. The burning cars set fire to those untouched by the explosion. The staff convoy consisting of seventy people was totally destroyed. Of our entire division only seventeen wagons survived. General Kappel presently gave orders to the officials to detach the surviving cars and to take them out of the inferno. It is not known if this explosion was the work of Bolsheviks or due to carelessness, but it disrupted everything and put new burdens on General Kappel."

In the aftermath of that Achinsk explosion I remember a particular encounter. Mama had been commissioned to take some medical supplies to the Red Cross train, and as I refused to be parted from her, iw as taken along.

The network of tracks was thickly filled with trains, but beyond them on the snowy plains campfires were burning and many tents were set up. Sleighs with horses stood around, hastily bandaged human beings moved as if in a daze, harassed grim aides and nurses came and went. There was confusion, despair and bewilderment. The skies were darkly leaden and the flickering flames of the campfires illuminated everything with a sinister unreal light. It was a fearful scene, more fearful than any I had ever witnessed.

A middle-aged woman with a Red Cross badge pinned to her coat approached Mama. She was leading a young girl of about sixteen wrapped in an over-sized gray squirrel coat. The girl's face was pitted with small bloody scars and her large eyes had a dazed unseeing look. The woman explained that the girl had been hurled out of her wagon by the explosion and was searching for her parents or someone who knew her. She could not remember her own name and could not recognize anyone. The Red Cross lady was trying to help. It hurt me to look at the girl, and I hid my face against Mama's coat as they talked.

Delivering her basket of supplies to the office of the Red Cross train, Mama hastily turned back with me to our own car. "Auntie" met us at the door and helped us climb in.

"Spared by God," Mama said, "but scared by the sight!"

The meaning of that came to me much later, for the memory of those bivouacs of agony have never faded from my mind.

# THE ODYSSEY OF
# UNCERTAINTY

After the debacle at Achinsk, it became increasingly difficult for my father to maintain the leadership and the organization of our echelon. In general, the Czech allies wanting to assert themselves and seeking their own political gains, were frequently ruthless in their dealings with the evacuees. They seized for their own use the engines of echelons bearing wounded men and fugitives, abandoning the unfortunates or evicting them from wagons when entire trains were needed. There are many stories of atrocities perpetrated by them for their own advantages, and it is not my purpose to relate the horrors, which came to our ears and surrounded us at close range. Every war, every revolution is hideous—in the end no war lords escape without scars, no winds of war blow without ill effects, and the people caught in these gales suffer most of all.

It was obvious that our echelon would hav eto be disbanded. Papa did the best he could to aid the people remaining in his care, helping them to secure other passages and the like. Only when the last group was accounted for did he turn to the problem of our own survival. With his Czech and Serbian passes and documents, and with the surreptitious aid of men who, though obeying orders from their superiors, were still well-disposed toward him, he was able to transfer us from one Czech train to another, and still another—all headed eastward. This odyssey is retained in memory by erratic flashbacks, all of them having the common denominator of great uncertainty and arduous effort.

There were freight cars where we had bunks on lower drafty berths, there were others high up near roofs where cracks of daylight were visible, and once below a small rectangular window glazed with rime. Sometimes the three of us bunked together, huddling on ill-assorted boards. The trains were stationary for long periods of time at some terminals. The mess wagon doled out meals, containers filled with what passed for stew and fried crullers called "knedliki." Sometimes there was coarse dark bread and sometimes thin pancakes filled with potatoes or cabbage. Milk had to be bought from the villagers who no longer came up to the trains with their wares.

There were some recuperating lightly wounded Czech soldiers in the cars with us, but few women evacuees. I don't remember any children. Some of the Czech soldiers riding with us were kind—I recall one who caught me scribbling with my colored pencils, and drew animals for me, dressing them up in fancy clothes. He had studied painting once, he told us, and described some pictures he had done back home.

Another man, nursing a broken arm, used to give me small cards with pictures of birds, which were found in packets of cigarettes that they all smoked. There was a man with a huge bristling moustache who could make it wiggle in order to get a laugh out of me. He told Mama I resembled his little daughter back home. At some station where we stood for many days, he found time to fashion me a little toy flatiron. When he was leaving to be transferred to another train, he enveloped me in a hug and begged me not to forget the "Old Cockroach," as the other men called him.

There were many uncertainties and hazards. Mama and a couple of women made several rips to some official's car to beg him to hook on an estra wagon for the evacuees. Mama made friends with the Russian mistress of a Czech commandant who agreed to take us on. A Czech doctor, in order not to part us, certified my father as suffering the effects of his former wounds, and gave him a berth in the infirmary. We stood in lines, we slept in our wraps, and we didn't know if our one trunk had been lost or not. We used to push it across tracks as we went seeking transportation. I trudged along with my parents and sometimes Papa carried me. We spoke little, sometime we all felt great despair. A Red Cross woman in charge of abandoned and homeless children offered to take me as far as the city of Chita where my parents would later join me, but we could not be separated even when things looked very dark indeed. We were three and we had to be together.

The Russian mistress of the Czech official confided to Mama that he was willing to marry her. "If you can help me alter some clothes, I will help you stay on."

By the dim candle lamp in her bunk Mama sat altering some fine looking garments. Starved for the sight of something pretty I admired them, fingering the lace. Mama jerked them out of my hands.

"Stolen loot," she murmured.

I also admired a gold, richly brocaded armchair brought into the car by someone. It looked incongruous amid the drab and crude surroundings.

"Stolen loot!"

The Cxech official and his mistress were duly married, and the young woman seemed very pleased with her altered garments. However, she denied Mama's request for a few drops of oil of cloves to mitigate an aching tooth, which had started to plague me. She explained that she had no authority to dole out medical supplies. I don't know how it was that I never became ill or suffered any colds. There were outbreaks and epidemics of typhoid fever and other communicable diseases, but mercifully they passed us by.

Grim, dreary, hungry days—a world of endless tracks and trains. I was no longer afraid of them, but learned to duck under the wagons in order to cross over. The cigarette cards of the birds that the wounded Cxech gave me were the only bright bits of color in a universe drained of all color. I used to spread them out and study them. Then Mama found a few skeins of bright embroidery floss in her valise, some scraps of canvas, and set me to cross-stitching some simple designs. The man who drwe dressed-up animals admired my skill and I stitched him his initials on a tiny bit of canvas, which he placed in his passport. Another soldier asked if I wuld do the same for him, and soon I was cross-stitching every-body's initials on tiny canvas scraps until the canvas gave out. A Red Cross orderly brought me a bit of bandaging gauze to stitch, but it did not work out very well.

The men in the wagon seemed to know that my father was a high-ranking evacuee, but they deferred to him without engaging him in conversation by offer-ing him an occasional cigarette, by stepping aside politely to let him pass, or by giving him a boost when he climbed into the car from the platform. They helped Mama and me by helping us down from the car and back up Averting their eyes they sometimes passed some; bits of information to Papa as casually as possible, almost without moving their lips. I understood by this time that although the Czech allies, our former "brothers," were no longer willing to champion our cause. Yet there were good and compassionate men among them.

At some station along the route some honey was distributed along with the usual dinner. Several; of the men brought their share of honeycombs to my mother, claiming that they had no taste for sweets. But my artist friend, along with honey, had a real treat for me. In one of the trains containing a large detach-ment of Czech soldiers, there was a pet bear, a real, live bear! The soldiers had taught him many tricks, and it was to see this bear that Mama and I were escorted across the railroad tracks, ducking under standing wagons as we went. The bear was indeed a wonder! Standing up as tall as the tallest soldier, he walked swaying up and down on his hind legs, danced to the tune of a harmonica, bowed engag-ingly with a paw on his heart, and engaged in a wrestling match with one man. He felled him to the ground and stood over him like a conqueror. He was given a bit of honeycomb from time to time, which he sucked ecstatically and demanded more by pawing at the pockets of laughing men. It was said that he was trained to stand in line for dinner with a pail over his paw and if anyone tried to get ahead of him, he would tumble the man to the ground. It was evident that he was a great favorite and provided much entertainment for men who needed an occasion to laugh. I loved that bear, of course, especially when he danced and bowed.

We continued to travel estward toward the city of Chita in the province of Zabaikal, having glimpsed from our car the mountain ranges and the great Lake Baikal, the deepest in the world. The weather had become very mild in that region, and as we passed the mountains the men opened the central doors of the car. They barricaded the lower part of the aperture with a couple of loose boards and then crowded around to watch the impressive scenery. My mother had been resting in our bunk, but Papa coaxed her to come down and the men made a place for her. I think she was quite worn out, and her sadness communicated itself to me as I watched her supporting herself slightly against Papa. He was trying to divert her by pointing out the grandeur of the mountains. Their togetherness made me think of the time I saw them reflected in the pier glass in Semipalatinsk when he fastened the necklace of pearls at her throat. I wanted very much to join them, but just then one of the men picked me up and held me so that I could have a better view. He was kind and I sensed his pleasure in holding me. For that reason I settled down more comfortably in his arms and watched the magnificent mountains.

We had been in transit three months since we left Semipalatinsk, and it seemed that we had been travelling for years. The world we left behind seemed at times very remote and unreal. From Chita, which already harbored many Russian refugees, Papa planned to make way to Harbin, Manchuria. The Russian Mission there was headed by a priest that he knew well. If only we could reach Chita safely! We considered ourselves fortunate to have survived the perils that far. The explosion at Achinsk had spared us—God's will again!—Even our trunk was still somewhere in the baggage car of our train. Mishka was in it! One day I would have Mishka with me again!

There was a man in the eschelon who acted as general manager. He was a Czech named Chigak. Shifty-eyed, important, he was brusque and intolerant of the evacuees, treating them with disdain or ignoring them entirely. He even short-rationed them whenever possible. He was not popular even with his own men, and the evacuees avoided him like the plague. Papa, warned by some sources, made himself very scarce whenever Chigak was around. Our senses in those days were so attuned to the nuances of every danger, and we were like forest animals in our instinctive reactions to sights and sounds. That sensitivity, developed so early in my life has also served me well. Those who have really known and loved me have called it perceptiveness. I call it instinct, born in desolate winter lands, nurtured among uncertainty and fear.

To get on with my tale—one night all three of us were sound asleep in our berth when the jolting train made a stop at some station. Papa was on the outside fo the berth, I was next to him and Mama against the wall. It was quiet in the wagon, all the men were resting, the dim light of one kerosene lamp swaying from the ceiling. Suddenly the doors were slid open and cold air rushed in. Up climbed an officer in the Red Army uniform. Chigak was close behind him.

"Passports please!" said the Red officer in a loud voice, shining a lantern about him. "Passports, please!" and made straight for our berth.

"Passport—papers" he repeated, reaching up to touch my father's shoulder.

Up came Papa on an elbow, blinking at the lantern light. With curses and oaths in pure Serbian because he knew no other words but vulgar ones in that language, he produced from his shirt pocket a stack of papers. I raised my head and whimpered at the light, then Mama woke. Papa continued to curse in Serbian. The officer's lantern swept over us, and he asked, "Wife and child?" Papa nodded. Then the officer said, "Excuse me.—All in order!" He handed Papa back his papers and went on to examine half-heartedly the paper of the waking men below.

They were gone in a few minutes and the doors slid shut. There was complete silence in the wagon. Slowly the men stirred. A candle was lit here and there. They looked up at us, but no one spoke. Finally the artist got out of his bunk and came up to Papa.

"They went straight up to you," he muttered. "I was awake. I saw it."

The train went on. Nothing was said the next morning, but there was present a kind of silent jubilation, as though these men were glad that no harm, no violence had come to pass to one among them. For years and we discussed it all—how it was that, awakened from sound sleep, Papa had the presence of mind to curse in Serbian while producing his papers? How it was that my whimpers showed Papa to be the very family man travelling with his wife and child mentioned in his falsified documents?

The rest of the journey was long, tedious, always on the periphery of peril and unease, but unmarked by any dramatic events. We arrived in snowy Chita one gray murky dawn that promised no sunrise. Bidding farewells to the men who rose up from their bunks to clasp our hands with unfeigned regret, we made our way to the baggage wagon supervised by the surly Chigak. That he was reluctant to hand over our trunk to us wa svery evident, but in the presence of some other officials he could not do otherwise. Moreover, it matched the description in

Papa's papers and was easily identified. Dumping it unceremoniously from the car upon the snow, Chigak turned away and, mercifully, we saw him no more.

We stood by the wagons not knowing what to do next. The station was nothing but a crude shed with few people moving among bundles and valises. There were no porters, but some men pulling sleds were offering to take our baggage to whatever destination.

An elderly man in a shabby coat and fur hat approached us drawing a sled by a rope. He indicated our trunk, mentioned some sum, and Papa nodded a reply. This terminal was some distance from the city proper, the man told us. Only freight trains stopped here, passenger trains used to go up to the city station. He could take us to a hostelry, one verst up the road where we could make some arrangements. Papa fumbled with his papers in the dim light, trying to find a certain address. I noticed that his hands were shaking. The man pulled out a box of matches, struck one, and sheltering it with one hand held it over ht papers so that Papa could see.

"Don't hurry—take your time—take your time," he repeated. His speech was clear and cultured, the match briefly illuminated a gaunt intelligent face, and his sunken eyes surveyed us with compassion. Swooping me up in one movement, he placed me on top of the trunk, picked up the rope, and started forward, my parents trudging behind. It had started to sleet and the pellets of ice stung our faces. The road was rutted with snow, deep drifts of it lay on either side. Thus we arrived in Chita.

# THE CHITA INTERLUDE

Chita, as a city, I don't remember at all except for the area where we stayed. We had arrived at the end of winter and spent spring and most of the summer there before going on to Harbin, China. We found quarters with a former officer of Papa's acquaintance. Having resigned from the military, the former Captain Kostin and his family established a residence in Chita and were able to aid many refugees who arrived later. My parents knew the Kostins in Omsk, where the wife had a dressmaking establishment, which the ladies of the regiment patronized. Even here she managed to do some work for the only clothing emporium in the city.

Madame Kostina, as everyone called her, was a very active enterprising woman. She was the mother of two boys—Toly (Anatole) my age, and an insufferable younger brat called Alex. Toly was a pleasant friendly boy, but his younger brother's mission in life was to make everyone miserable. Gifted with a vivid imagination he played mean pranks on the kitchen help, was totally immune to the frequent wallopings his father administered, took delight in teasing his good-natured brother, and must have lain awake nights planning mischief. His mother, however, doted on him, the help shied away from him, and I learned quickly to keep out of his way. One of his chief delights was to pee into people's boots if he found them standing around, or to release bottled roaches in beds and sofas. By today's high-minded child psychologists, he would be called hyperactive. By our standards he was an incorrigible nasty little boy.

The house where we occupied one room with kitchen privileges was a rabbit-arren of a place with many rooms, unexpected staircases, corridors and passageways. Directly across the narrow street stood a small Catholic Church fronted by a ting graveyard. It was surrounded by a wooden fence and had some shrubs and acacia trees. I remember it well because Papa became friendly with the priest and his younger brother and used to go over to chat with them, often taking me along. In early evenings they would sit outside on one of the branches by the tombstones and converse, while I wandered around looking at the blackended, crumbling memorials. I liked reading the names and inscriptions. The priest had a library of Russian and Polish books which Papa borrowed from time to time.

Most of them were classics and historical novels familiar to Papa, but to divert his mind from constant encrochments of the very recent past, he tried to escape into their pages. I also frequently dipped into them, not quite understanding, but fascinated by the strange names and the mention of a certain diamond necklace. Years later, savoring the enchantment of the Dumas novels, I realized that In Chita, I had been reading the Russain translation of "The Queen's Necklace."

Madame Kostina lost no time in finding some embroidery work for Mama in the emporium, and Papa went about selling some of our things and investigating the possibilities of travel to Harbin.

Toly and I got along very well together, and soemtimes earned a special tid-bit from the gaunt, grim-faced cook who ruled the kitchen and referred to Toly's brother as "Satan's spawn." Although the unfortunate Alex often ruins our games and made a nuisance of himself, he loved to sing, and always joined us when we marched around the dining table singing, "Over the Blue Ocean Waves"—a most maudlin ballad involving a ghost ship and the Emperor Napoleon.

When a teacher was engaged for Toly, Mama thoguht that I, too, should resume studies, and twice a week we had lessons with a very stout middle-aged woman who had been a teacher of elementary grades in some gymnasia. She was nothing like my beloved Margarita Ivanovna, although she was pleasant and easy-going. Her mind, however, was on her own problems of survival, and she taught half-heartedly. I was way ahead of Toly in most studies, and while he applied himself earnestly, I was just as earnestly bored. It was fortunate that the teacher, whose name I've forgotten, noted my lassitude and suggested that I should begin a kind of daily journal, recording events. That did not appeal to me, but I did start writing a documentary of my Mishka's adverntures—how he had lived with me, how he traveled in a trunk, and so on. He and I had been happily reunited when we arrived in Chita and the trunk was unpacked. So, while Toly was struggling with his sums, I began the saga of my beloved bear. This was my first vernture into composition, and I enjoyed it. I don't know by what miracle that diary of a toy bear survived, but it did, and I still have it.

Madame Kostina, deploring the fact that her children were boys, gave Mama some material for a few dresses for me and was pleased to see me in new clothes. The blue, fur-lined coat, worn throughout the echelon journey was given away to someone after the documents that it secreted had been removed.

Our stay in Chita was far longer than we arnticipated, but we knew that we would be moving on eventually. Harbin was to be the destination, and Papa spent much time in making contacts with the mission tehre. Although Toly's friendship and frank admiration were rewarding, I, solitary child that I was, felt quite detached from any bonds. Mama and Papa and I were an entity—separated from the rest by the experiences we went through together. I think we were emotionally drained and totally exhausted after our wintertime train ride. The colorless environment in Chita, which did not provide any particular beneficent restoratives, did not give us an opportunity to draw a breath. Too much had yet to be done; too many plans and problems to be considered. We did not talk and could not yet talk about forward movement with an echelon. When persistent images flitted through my mind, I pushed them away or sang louder to drown out the rattle of the ghost train. In that drab city of Chita years ago, I said it before Scarlet O'Hara even thought of it, "I'll think about that tomorrow."

# *HARBIN*

How we reached Harbin I do not remember, but there we had a refuge at the Russian Mission established many years earlier. The head at that time was Father Alexander Shabashev who had been close to my father in Omsk. He helped and harbored other Russian refugess. And later made his way to America.

The Mission contained a church in the traditional architectural style, a parish house, and several large buildings—all these within a huge courtyard. A convent and a monastery existed together side by side. Before the Revoution this would not have been possible. The parish house harbored many refugees, sometimes so crowded that many slept on pallets on dinning and living room floors. Many of the refugees were high-ranking officials of military and civilian circles. All of them were making a temporary stay at the Mission while fleeing to a safer haven. Father Shabashev was kept very busy. His wife was not with him as he had dispatched her to some relatives. My mother, for the time, became his official hostess.

We occupied one crowded room in the parish. It had been a study and was crammed with books. There was a communal bathroom and dining-room. People came and went. Some stayed for a while. Therewas also an archbishop, hounded out of Russia and now living with monastery brothers. In the convent part of the establishment there was a Mother Superior from some prestigious convent in Russia.

Arrangements for travel to America too time. My father had to work for necessary funds, so we stayed at the Mission for several months. It was there that I was enrolled in a gymnasia.

Father Shabashev was a huge bear of a man who knew his way around, juggling politics, badgering the Chinese officials, throwing his clerical weight around in order to aid the refugees who came in an endless stream. There were families with children, there were wives separated by the Revolution from their husbands, there were single men with only themselves to look after. There was, for instance, an elderly general with an eye out for younger women. There was another younger general who tried to seduce the refugee wives. They all gathered at the dinner table and played endless card games after dinner. An observant child saw many things, which were understood only in later years.

There were some Chinese converts who worked about the place. The cook was one, but he "lost face" when my mother was asked to accompany him to the produce market because it was thought that he cheated. Some russian families lived in the city and gathered at the mission on Sundays.

Father Shabashev was fond of me, called me "Martyn" for some reason, and granted permission to sing in the church choir on Sundays. On those days I stood with the choir on the eleveated platform to one side of the altar and opened my mouth to whatever I knew of chants and hymns. I also made a friend, a Brother Gregory, who had a wooden leg and liked to draw. My drawing was encouraged by him. Sitting out in the courtyard he would draw buildings, trees, grasses and would make me draw also. He had pads of drawing paper, which he would share with me. He showed me how one could make thick and thin lines, rub in shadows and make things appear "near" and "far." In other words, he began my perception of perspective.

At the Mission I attended many weddings but also there was my first glimpse of death. At a nearby village a young child was killed by a bomb while playing outdoors. The funeral was at the Mission. I had a glimpse of the waxen-faced child in a small coffin and I remember for a long while the wails of her heart-broken mother:

"They killed her! They killed my little girl!"

A maintenance man with a family of children lived at the Mission. A little girl, my age, called Fatina sometimes played with me. She was a friendly, pleasant child, and when she went away to visit some relatives, I missed her. She came bck a couple of weeks later and called out, "I'm back, and I brought you a present." I don't remember what it was, but I do recall her sunny disposition and her willingness to play whatever game I proposed. She wass, I thik, a little in awe of my parents and Father Shabashev. Although he always was very kind to her, patted her on the head as eh went by and gave her a share of fruits, which the parishioners often brought him. Speaking of fruits, it was in Harbin that I tasted my first banana.

The archbishop, a venerable old man who looked like one of the saints on the church panels, sometimes took walks in the courtyard, and invited me to walk with him. One always approached him with folded hands, asking for a blessing. After that one could talk wnad walk. I think I amused him. He asked me about my studies and made me talk. Once he pulled out a huge pear from the depths of his cassock and gave it to me.

There were not many trees in the courtyard, but there were some areas of uncut grass. The grass must have been timothy. I recall its particular fragrance drawn out by the sun. In another country in another age the timothty grass brought back the Harbin courtyard.

The sisters of the convent, going about in their black robes, aroused my curiosity. One of them was a young woman with huge eyes in a gaunt face, and sometimes she read aloud at the church services. She had wonderful voice and enunciated words with a particular clarity.

Among the monks there was one who had a weakness for drink and sometimes drank himself into a stupor. The following day he would appear grim-faced and sullen in the choir. I'm afraid I stared at him more than I should have.

I recall playing with some children of the refugee families, but there were no real friendships. There was a general's daughter called "Milochka," and also there was a little boy who accidentally wounded me with a small rock as we were playing. The sight of blood pouring from my head scared him senseless, and my parents had a hard time persuading him that it was "all right" and that I would live.

To supplement funds necessary for travel to America, my father worked as a manager of a mill in a nearby Chinese village. He was the only white man there, and I recall that my mother and I once went to see the place. There were many workers, I remember, all of them wearing coolie hats and blue padded jackets. It was a very primitive place.

Father Shabashev eventually came to America where his wife joined him. I think he ended his days at a Russian mission in Canada.

# GYMNASIA—AND THE LAST FAREWELL

In Harbin I attended an gymnasia that was run on the old conservative lines approved in Russian before the revolution. It was attended by the daughters of persons whose fortunes had brought them to that part of the world. Its staff was composed of instructors from some of the most prestigious Russian schools of the old regime.

I understand that my father paid for my entry fees with gold coins and took me to the examining board to determine into which class I would be placed. Both he and Mama hoped it would be First Class, not the "preparatory" one.

I remember something of that examination where my knowledge was tested. In grammar I was requested to write in dictation the phrase—Otets Roobit drova—(Father is chopping wood)—and the examining teacher looked approvingly at the sentence and siad to someone, "Look how well she writes!" Also I was praised for my clear diction and ability to read. I made the First Class, and there was much jubilation. My dear Margarita Ivanovna must have given me a sound foundation.

The gymnasia building to which I walked several long city blocks every morning was strark and official looking. My classroom, containing some twenty girls, had desks accomodating two students at each, and opened out on a balcony. There was a large blackboard, a raised dais with a desk for the teacher, a large globe on a stand, and an icon with a lighted virgil lamp in one corner. A "class-dame"—presided over each classroom, She was sort of a home room teacher. We wore brown dresses with black aprons, but there were no strict regulations about the styles.

Of the teachers, I remember well the "class-dame" who entered our grades into a journal every day. Everyone liked her. She was a middle-aged lady who dealt with us gently but firmly, and we respected and tried to please her. There was an elderly minister who came weekly for religious instruction. The several Jewish girls in our class had their own rabbi, but sometimes both men got together and gave us talks on the history of religion. I remember our priest telling

111

us to be respectful of all faiths and encouraging us to be tolerant of all beliefs, many of which contained great wisdom.

There was a lady who taught grammar and literature who called on me time and again to read passages aloud to the class. For her I memorized poems beyond the given assignments, and was more rewarded by her warm smile than by the high grades she gave me. There was also the geography teacher, a high-bosomed very dignified lady of whom we were all in awe. I think she had taught earlier at the Smolny Institute in St. Petersburg. All of these instructors, coming, as I mentioned, from outstanding institutions, were used to good manners and good behavior from their students and for the most part were not disappointed in their expectations. Of course there were pranks, harmless for the most part and lapses of "lady-like" decorum, but these matters were dealt with great dignity.

One recess, going down the stairs that led to the recreation hall, I saw through a window that looked out on an enclosed courtyard, a huge white bearskin placed on a trestle for an airing.

"Bear! Bear! Bear," I shrieked, skipping down, and was apprehended by one of the "class-dames." I was made to return to my own classroom and stand in front of the blackboard. So the next class in geography found me there.

"And how have you distinguished yourself, young lady?" asked the dignified geography teacher, looking down her rather prominent nose.

"I was running downstairs and yelling 'Bear! Bear! Bear!'"

"Commendable!" sniffed the lady, turning away, but not before I noted that her mouth twitched, changing the habitually frowning line.

The same lady, I observed, had an entirely different relationiship with the older girls of the Upper Class. Once, because their own classroom was, for some reason, temporarily unavailable, they came in a group to have their geography lesson in our room during our study-period, and we, the younger ones, were privileged to see how those young ladies whom we envied conducted themselves with our awe-inspiring mentor. We noted the difference at once. How free and uninhibited they were with her! How teasing were their amiles as they cajoled her not to give them a long assignment over the weekend. And she, without losing her dignity, looked upon them with tolerance, even with some fondness, and conceded grudgingly that perhaps a long assignment "would strain their mental capacity."

Drawing, dancing, needlework and music had to be omitted from the curriculum, but during our recess periods in the recreation hall, one of the younger teachers sometimes gathered us together. Then, if someone could be found to play the piano which stood in one corner of the hall, she would teach us some steps of the old mazurka or a polka.

The Headmistress of the school, a tall, willowy aristocrat, sometimes came into the hall to see us dance when she heard the music. She would stand, nodding approvingly as we tried to imitate the teacher. She was quite handsome with dark piled-up hair and great velvety dark eyes. I heard Papa telling Mama that she was a real "krassavitsa' (a beauty) and added that her figure was excellent. Mama replied that it was too bad he could not enroll at the gymnasia for a refresher course.

I don't recall forming any friendships for I was there a very short period. I recall the girls were pleasant and mannerly, but no particular faces stand out. The entire environment was a totally new experience that absorbed me completely. Although I was by no means an outstanding student, I got along fairly well. During our stay in Harbin, every effort was made to contact my uncle in America and to leave for the US as soon as possible.

I knew that this time the long journey would involve sailing, and I looked and looked at the great globe that stood in the classroom with its blue expanse of the oceans. I remebered the steamship that took me from Omsk to the village of Evgoschino, and faces drifted over the globe—Vasilisa Ivanovna, the Kaliznikovs, Margarita Ivanovna, little Yuri—and my own grandmother. The blue ocean areas blurred with the continents and I spun the globe again and again. Even at that age I was dimly aware that a part of my life had come to a close.

Then one day I was walking the long school corridor to the study of the Headmistress. I had been instructed to say goodbye to her personally, even though Papa had been in to see her previously. I had never been in her study before. I knocked on the panel door and was told to enter. I was suddenly in a large lofty room, feeling very small.

The Headmistress sat behind a huge desk and looked at me searchingly as I hesitated. "Yes?" she said, "what is it?

"We are going to America," I blurted out.

She smiled, rose, and came toward me.

"And you have come to say goodbye, yes?" she stretched out her hand.

"Yes."

"So, American is a long, long way off. I wish you a safe yourney."

I thanked her and slowly backed away. She smiled again as she watched me with her magnificent eyes.

At the door I stopped and made my final curtsey, which was painstakingly low. Very, very low!

# SOME IMPRESSIONS OF JAPAN

Once we left our ship from China, we traveled on trains through a countryside where gentle warm rain fell over rice fields and houses on stilts. The scenery was exactly as depicted in Japanese prints.

The trains had benches facing each other lengthwise so that one always sat facing other people. There were families with children, lone travelers and serious-faced male students in sombre garb. They opened their books as soon as they were seated and immersed themselves in study, rarely looking up.

My father relieved the tedium of our travel by purchasing small inflatable tissue-paper balls, which we blew up and tossed to each other. I had never seen them before. Some would, naturally, fly across the aisle and be sent back to us by willing hands. Eventually there would be a real game with people on opposite seats batting back and forth a multicolored tissue-paper ball. Sometimes the ball would bounce on the book of a studying student, but he would brush it aside as on would a pesky gnat. Then if it came again on him, he would direct a more purposeful slap. Finally, however, he would close his book, tuck it away, and join wholeheartedly in the play. This happened many times.

Once in a while a vendor would come through selling tangerines in bags of knotted twine. I learned to love them and I enjoyed peeling their fragrant skins. Everyone was friendly and courteous and most attentive. Small children, looking like porcelain dolls in their colorful kimonos, bowed and nodded, and when my parents offered them bars of chocolate they were encouraged by their own parents to offer me their own sweet, strange-tasting candy. Tiny tots handled chopsticks with great dexterity when eating rice out of small wooden boxes. I marveled how they did it, for try as I would, I could not handle chopsticks.

At that time not many people were wearing European clothes, although there were men in Western tailored suits. The women, however, were always in kimonos, some with magnificent obis, and their lacquered intricate hairstyles were enchanting. Many of them used make-up in the traditional way and their faces were like exquisite masks of porcelain. It was delightful to view them when they gathered together, bowing to each other and gracefully gesticulating.

The passage through Japan remains in my mind like something of a dream. I recall misty landscapes and slanting gentle rain that caused no inconvenience; it was a kind of a caress, giving substance to a story-book land. It was like living in a Japanese print.

As people, the Japanese were very friendly. I remember how they smiled at the foreign child with a golden teddy-bear cluched in her arms. Sometimes they stopped and stroked my Mishka. I never drew away, and when the little children stretched their chubby hands toward him, I would hold him out, allowing him to be petted. For their sake, I would press his belly so that he would "growl" for their delight. I recall that Mama once prompted me to curtsey to some Japanese man who had a large family At once his children responded with ceremonial bows, and I curtseyed again, and they bowed again. The exchange went on for some time.

In Yokohama we wondered through the market places and my parents bought me a Japanese doll, and a little box with a doll and six wigs, which were to be worn at different stages of maturity. I still have that box, and I still wear the gold-and-black cufflinks that my father purchased. My parents had little money to spend, but we did acquire a few souvenirs. We were enchanted with the colorful country after our experiences of fleeing from Russia.

It was in Tokyo that we awaited our visas and passages to America. The nightmares of the Revolution, if not fading, were behind us. We were no longer the hunted or the pursued. The beauty and graciousness of Japan must have been like a temporary balm over the hearts of my parents aching for their own country. It is my conviction that the ache never abated in all the years that they lived in America. They must have been most gallant and courageous young people at the time. I remember them laughing with tears in their eyes. It seemed that they tried to take in all the beauty of another country that gave them refuge and in doing so they tried giving me a memorable time to make up for all our former trials.

We rode in rickshaws, Mama and I in one and Papa by himself in another. On some trip Papa's rickshaw-man was an emaciated, coughing individual. Papa tried talking to him because he wanted the experience of pulling the vehicle. However, when he tried, he found that he could make only a few steps. The rickshaw-man was trained to a certain dog-trot, which made the carriage flow smoothly. Papa paid him double and seated himself in the rickshaw, defeated. They had no common language, but Papa said, "I think he understood. He put his hand over mine and his eyes went deep into mine."

We went into a movie house and had cloth slippers placed over our shoes. We half-reclined on benches watching a screen where some drama was taking place. A man with a huge book sat beneath the screen and read out the dialogue, tapping a stick from time to time to simulate the action.

It is different there now. Japan is a modern country. I am thankful that in my time I passed through the kind of landscape that one finds only on old Japanese prints. Sometimes the scent of a tangerine brings up a memory—I see rice fields, pagodas, cranes wringing their way over marshes, small bridges with pedestrians hurrying over them and the wonderful, warm, slanting, caressing rain.

# THE KINDNESS OF TWO
# YOUNG PEOPLE IN JAPAN

The years have not dimmed the memory of two young people, one Japanese, the other Russian, both teenagers. To them I owe an everlasting debt of gratitude for a feeling of security and care, which they imparted by their goodwill and kindness. I have often wondered what became of them, and I always wished them well and hoped good fortune would come their way.

Before reaching Yokohama there were several stops in some now-forgotten towns, and one stop was in a hotel managed by some Russians. There arose some difficulty in locating the baggage, which traveled with us. Both my parents had to visit various bureaus in order to identify it. It was necessary to leave me at the hotel, and some arrangement was made with the staff to have me looked after while they were away.

The task fell to a young Russian teenager, a girl of about twelve or so, in whose care I was placed. I don't recall her appearance, but she had a way with small children, and I felt secure under her care. Most of the time was spent in a large court-yard where she played with me, reassuring me from time to time that indeed my parents would soon return, never leaving me, giving me all the attention and care I needed. It also developed, s time went on, that this day was her birthday.

I recall that some relatives arrived to celebrate and some aunt finally came out of the house calling her to come in. I remember that the aunt said, "Nina! Nina, why are you out here? Everyone is asking where is the birthday girl?"

I don't recall what Nina answered, but she did not forsake me. She stayed with me until my parents returned and left only when I was once more reunited with them. I don't know if my parents thanked her adequately, I only remember how I tagged after her all through the hours of her birthday because of my fear of being abandoned. She had a family waiting with presents and celebration, but she felt a storn sense of duty to a small, frightened child. I've thought of her often and blessed her many times.

In Yokohama, before we were to embark on our final journey to America, there was another hotel, which was managed by a Russian Jewish woman. She spoke beautiful Russian, was helpful to my parents with arrangements, and was something of a character. In her employ was a head housemaid, a plump motherly Katia, who was overjoyed to meet Russians like my parents and who could not do enough to make them comfortable. She imparted much information and reassurance and was very concerned about our welfare. She had under her all the hotel help.

Among her workers was a Japanese boy of about thirteen who ran errands, did some housework, and made himself generally useful. He was Katia's pet and she even taught him some Russian rhymes, which he declaimed in a sing-gong manner.

Again, while arrangements were being made, I was left much alone, but this time Katia's care and concern were so evident, that I did not have any feeling of insecurity or fear. The hotel was not large, but rooms were comfortable and I was looked after, even though there were periods when I was quite alone. At those times I remember venturing out of the room into the hall where the Japanese boy was sweeping and dusting the stairway. Always he waved a friendly hand and gave me a broad smile. He would tuck the feather duster in the pocket of his pants and slide down the banisters to amuse me. When he saw my delight, he would repeat the performance several times. He also recited jingles that Katia had taught him, then, at my command, he would slide down the banister again as I shrieked with laughter. Once Katia appeared from somewhere and shook her finger at him, but he went on sliding, grinning at my pleasure.

What happened to him, that moon-faced, happy Japanese boy who lit up that narrow, dark hall with is antics and made a lonely child laugh? Oh, to know! Across the years and oceans my heart goes out to him, whom I have never forgotten.

# EPILOGUE

We sailed to America on a liner called "Nile," and landed in San Francisco during the Christmas week, two days before the new Year. The "Nile" was not large, and the passage over wintry seas was rough at times. We traveled second-class and were frequently invited by the friendly first-class passengers to share in their theatricals and festivities. Sometimes we would see a movie with them. Everyone was most kind.

There was an American family of five small children and a very loyal elder brother, who supervised games, promenades on deck and created all sorts of activities. He must have been about sixteen, a pleasant-faced boy with unlimited patience and tact. By gestures and mimic he translated our desires to each other since we knew no English. Yet he taught me to play the card game "Casino," introduced me to my first olive, which I promptly spat out into a napkin, and relieved both his parents and mine by his ever-present attention and watchfulness.

I remember that the liner had narrow corridors with doors, doors, and doors. The dining salon sometimes had wooden frameworks on the tables to hold the plates in place. I remember passing a florist shop located in one of the corridors and the sight of fresh flowers, roses mainly, behind the glass refrigerator doors seemed strange and out of place. Outside the sea was a mass of restless gray-green water blending into the leaden sky.

I think I was a little nauseated the first couple of days, then recovered quickly. Our steward was a moon-faced, smiling Chinaman who brought me segments of grapefruit and oranges, and urged me to go and join the American children. I don't remember what my parents did during the passage.

Certain passengers flash through my mind. There was a young Russian woman who was traveling with her new American husband. There were some American men interested in Russian history who came at intervals to talk to Papa in broken Russian. The American family with children had a most pleasant mother and father. I recall both of them engaging my parents in conversation with the help of a Russian-English dictionary. The mother, always knitting something let it be known that the length of cherry-colored wool, rapidly growing under her nimble fingers, was intended as a sweater for me. Whereupon Mama, not to be outdone, promptly set to embroidering the one towel she had brought for handwork, with the initials of the family. Kindness, freedom from apprehension and fears were new experiences for us.

Cables from Captain Brady in San Francisco and Papa's brother in Baltimore were delivered personally to our cabin by one of the ship's officers who knew a bit of Russian. He visited us time and again, pouring over Papas papers and photos and lingering for long conversations. I remember his attentive and respectful mien, saluting Papa as he entered and accepting a tiny glass of cognac from the bottle that Papa treasured.

There were good days of comradeship and some bad nights with winter storms. Yet we reached San Francisco safely, said goodbyes to the kind people who had aided our pasage, and prepared to go ashore. Some reporters came to interview Papa, and eh gave them a few brief statements though interpreters.

Then, suddenly, Captain Grady came down the deck with his attractive young wife. He held his arms wife open in greeting, yet he looked different in civilian clothes. He embraced all three of us. No words were spoken. He stood back a little facing Papa and snapped open the collar of his shirt. Around his neck, instead of the medallion of Lucifer, was Papa's gold baptismal cross!

# MY RETURN—AFTER FIFTY YEARS

In November 1988 I returned to my native land. My surprises were immediate. Where were the horses and carriages, the store windows filled with beautiful things, the fashionable ladies and the handsomely-dressed gentlemen? It was not the Russia I had known in my youth. It was another world, more like the frightening Russia of my last year there. Streets and buildings were drab, people badly dressed and the food in the restaurants of poor quality. Moscow and St. Petersburg were a disappointment. The grand palaces and monuments could only remind me of the Russia I lost.

Yet it was on a trip up the Volga River that I found some of the Russia that I remembered so well. It was a thrill to be sailing along the waters where my grand uncle General Kappel achieved his outstanding victories over the Bolsheviks. How clever he was in freeing one city after another. Once when the Reds had laid a trap for him on the Volga, he conjured a train and took his men around the waiting enemy. Unfortunately events and lack of supplies forced his retreat into Siberia. It was there that I would have met him had there not been the terrible explosion in Atchinsk.

Russian village girls from towns along the Volga served as waitresses on the ship. Talking with them, and they were always thrilled that an American spoke Russian, I learned that the Russians in the outer areas were still my kin. They were religious, they were thoughtful and they had not lost the Russian joie de vivre. One very plain, but terribly sweet young lady even brought me a string of booblichki as a gift after we stopped at a small village. Her kindness warmed my heart and told me that the Russian soul was still very much a reality and a gift from God.

Mishka and Me

Grandmother

Papa

Mama

0-595-30408-7

Made in the USA
Lexington, KY
09 April 2013